POEMS BY DESIGN

INSPIRATION FOR ALL OCCASIONS

GLADYS KNEELAND

www.xulonpress.com

BIRTHDAYS

A LITTLE GIFT

I'M PRESENTING YOU A LITTLE GIFT,
BECAUSE YOU MEAN SO MUCH TO ME.
YOU'RE KIND, LOVING AND CARING
HOW ELSE COULD YOU BE?
GOD KNEW SOMEONE
WOULD NEED IT
AND THAT
SOMEONE INCLUDES ME.

THE LOVE YOU SHARE
COMES STRAIGHT FROM YOUR
HEART
GOD DESIGNED YOU THAT WAY
HE KNOWS THE END FROM THE START.

MY MOTHER IS GONE, BUT
GOD SENT YOU
WHAT AN AWSOME GOD,
HE KNEW I NEEDED THAT TOO.

I THANK GOD FOR YOU
NOT JUST TODAY,
I MENTION YOUR NAME WHEN
I KNEEL AND PRAY.
HAPPY THANKSGIVING MOTHER EASLEY
YOU'RE LIKE A BEAUTIFUL FLOWER

THAT CONTINUES TO BLOOM.
YOU'RE LIKE A SPECIAL ROSE
THAT LIGHTS UP A ROOM.

I PRAY SUNSHINE AND BLESSINGS
CONTINUE YOUR WAY,
I COULD GO ON AND ON BECAUSE THERE'S
SO MUCH TO SAY.

I THANK GOD FOR YOU IN MY LITTLE WAY
WITH A GREAT BIG HEART
EVERYDAY!

DEBBIE

A DELIGHT TO HER PARENTS
A BLESSING IN DISGUISE;
SHE MADE HER ENTRANCE
INTO THE WORLD
SURELY GOD WAS ON HER SIDE.

DEBORAH
A WARRIOR'S NAME,
IT FIT HER VERY WELL;
GOD'S BLESSINGS UPON HER;
IT WAS VERY PLAIN TO TELL.

EVERYONE CALLED HER DEBBIE
THROUGHOUT ALL THESE YEARS;
WITH SOME OF US SHE'S LAUGHED,
AND SOME SHE'S SHED TEARS.

DEBBIE GREW UP HERE
AND HERE SHE CHOSE TO STAY;
PEOPLE LATCHED ON TO HER,
A PIED PIPER YOU MIGHT SAY.
THE CHILDREN LOVED HER
THEY MADE HER VERY PROUD
WITH ANGELIC VOICES
SINGING GOD'S PRAISES LOUD.

ALWAYS WORKING HARD
FOR THE LORD
NO MATTER THE COST
SHE BELIEVES IN HER HEART,
NO SOUL SHOULD BE LOST.

TELLING EVERYONE SHE MEETS
ABOUT HIS SAVING GRACE;
GIVE YOUR HEART TO THE LORD
AND JOIN THIS CHRISTIAN RACE!!

NO MATTER THE JOB, SHE GOES
THE EXTRA MILE,
NO MATTER THE TASK, SHE ALWAYS WEARS A SMILE.
BUMPS, KNOCKS, AND KICKS SHE FACED
ALONG THE WAY,
BUT DEBBIE IS A WARRIOR, AND SHE KNOWS
HOW TO PRAY.

WEARING THE ARMOUR OF GOD,
THE SHIELD OF FAITH IN HER HAND
A SOLDIER IN GOD'S ARMY
HE GIVES HER STRENGTH TO STAND.

GOD IS NOT UNRIGHTEOUS
TO FORGET HER LABOR OF LOVE;
DISAPPOINTMENTS TRIED TO
STOP HER;
BUT THEY NEVER COULD

SHE BELIEVED ON HIS WORD
AND ON HIS PROMISES SHE STOOD.

EVERYONE KNOWS DEBBIE, SEEMS I CAN ALWAYS
HEAR HER SAY...
CAST YOUR BREAD UPON THE WATER
AND YOU WILL FIND IT AGAIN SOMEDAY.
60 YEARS OF HIS MERCY,
60 YEARS OF HIS GRACE;
SOMETIME THE WAR GOT FIERCE;
BUT NOTHING COULD SHAKE HER FAITH.

TODAY WE CELEBRATE DEBBIE;
SHE DESERVES MEDALS,
ACCOLADES AND ALL;
A MIGHTY SOLDIER IN THE ARMY;
ANSWERING GOD'S CALL.

DEBBIE

THE CAPTIAN OF THE ARMY IS PLEASED WITH HIS
WARRIOR TODAY;
BUT GIFTS, CARDS AND PRESENTS
WILL ALL FADE AWAY.
MATERIAL THINGS ARE TEMPORARY
FOR EVERYONE TO SEE;
BUT HER CROWN OF GLORY WILL LAST
THROUGHOUT ETERNITY!!

FORTY IS A BEAUTIFUL AGE

THANK YOU FOR ALLOWING ME TO SPEAK
INTO YOUR LIFE
TO SPEAK PEACE, NOT STRESS AND SURELY
NOT STRIFE.

<u>TO SPEAK OF GOD</u> YOU ALWAYS MAKE HIM
NUMBER ONE
BECAUSE OF HIS LOVE FOR YOU HE GAVE
HIS ONLY SON.
OPEN UP YOUR HEART AND LET GOD'S SPIRIT FLOW
THE LOVE YOU WILL EXPERIENCE IS MORE THAN
YOU WILL EVER KNOW.
GIVE ALL YOUR CARES TO HIM (AT FORTY)
JUST RELAX
WHEN YOU WAKE EVERY MORNING YOU KNOW WHO
HAS YOUR BACK.

<u>TO SPEAK OF HOME</u> THE BLESSING ON YOUR
CHILDREN, THE GIFTS GOD GAVE TO YOU
AND WHEN SOMEONE GIVES YOU A PRESENT, THANKS
IS WHAT YOU DO!
AT FORTY GONE ARE DIRTY DIAPERS, EVERY
RATTLE AND TOY
YOU KEEP YOUR HOME CLEAN ENOUGH TO
BE HEALTHY
AND MESSY ENOUGH TO ENJOY.

TO SPEAK OF WORK THE LORD WILL SUPPLY ALL
YOUR NEED ACCORDING TO HIS RICHES IN GLORY
COMMIT YOUR WORK TO HIM, AND SISTER DON'T
YOU WORRY.
TO SPEAK THE FAVOR OF GOD IN ALL YOU DO,
PROMOTION COMES FROM HIM, HE WILL SEE YOU
THROUGH. YOU DON'T GET INVOLVED IN GOSSIP AND
IDLE TALK OF OTHERS GOD GAVE US A COMMAND
TO LOVE OUR SISTERS AND OUR BROTHERS. GOD
JUDGES IN ALL WE DO, WHEN WE POINT A FINGER AT
SOMEONE, THREE IS POINTED BACK AT YOU.

TO SPEAK OF JOY LIVE EACH DAY TO THE FULLEST,
DON'T DWELL ON THE PAST. THINK ON THINGS
ABOVE, AND LOVE THAT WILL LAST. ENJOY ALL THE
BEAUTY GOD HAS SUPPLIED, TAKE A WALK, SEE A
MOVIE, TAKE A TRIP AND EVEN DO A DANCE; DON'T
WAIT UNTIL IT'S TO LATE, SO MANY NEVER GOT
THE CHANCE.

TO SPEAK OF REST AT FORTY GET ALL THE SLEEP
YOU CAN. SLAP ON ALL YOUR COLD CREAM TURN
OFF ALL THOSE LIGHTS, WHAT EVER WENT WRONG
TODAY, TOMORROW HE'LL MAKE IT RIGHT. REST
IN THE LORD, HOURS QUICKLY TURN TODAYS, HIS
ANGELS HAS CHARGE OVER YOU TO KEEP YOU IN
ALL YOUR WAYS.
AT FORTY YOU HAVE EXPERIENCED A LOT, IT'S A
TIME OF FEELING CONFIDENT, WALKING IN ALL GOD

HAS FOR YOU, DOORS OF OPPORTUNITY ARE OPEN
JUST WALK RIGHT THROUGH.
THINK ON PSALMS 92: THEY SHALL STILL BRING
FORTH FRUIT IN OLD AGE; GOD IS IN CONTROL, HE
HAS SET THE STAGE.
BE BOLD ABOUT YOUR DREAMS, PRAY YOUR DESIRES
COME TRUE. AT FORTY EMBRACE YOUR DESTINY,
GOD HAS GOOD THINGS IN STORE FOR YOU.

WE CELEBRATE YOU PASTOR JACKIE

50 YEARS OF GOD'S MERCY,
50 YEARS OF HIS GRACE
HOW CAN I DESCRIBE HER,
WHAT CAN I SAY…..?
ABOUNDING WITH GODLY WISDOM
SHE'S SO BLESSED THAT WAY.
SO POISED, SO GRACEFUL
EVERYONE CAN SEE
A JEWEL IN THE MASTER'S HANDS,
NO BETTER PLACE TO BE.
****

SHE TRULY LOVES HER
FAMILY AND FRIENDS
TRUSTING THE LORD TO KEEP THEM,
ON HIM SHE CAN DEPEND!
SHE'S AWARE HER TIME IS PRECIOUS
EACH YEAR SHE THAT LIVES
A SMILE AND KIND WORDS
ARE GIFTS SHE FREELY GIVES.
****

MORE TOLERANT OF OTHERS
AND THEIR SHORTCOMINGS TOO.
SHE KNOWS GOD CAN CHANGE A HEART,
HE MAKES ALL THINGS NEW.
BEFORE SHE CONDEMS,
SHE ALWAYS THINKS TWICE,

SHARING A HUG, AND SOME GODLY ADVICE.
MORE ACCEPTABLE OF THINGS SHE CANNOT CHANGE,
WHEN TRIALS ARISE,
SHE CALLS ON HIS NAME.
HUMBLY SHE SURRENDERS TO GOD'S HOLY WILL
SHE KNOWS THE VICTORY IS HERS,
IF SHE JUST KEEPS STILL.
****

INTOLERANT OF INJUSTICE AND UNFAIRNESS AS WELL,
PEOPLE FALL SHORT,
AND SOMETIMES THEY FAIL.
WITH HER LOVING HEART AND PRAYER
SHE TREATS OTHERS RIGHT,
THE BATTLE IS NOT HERS WHEN GOD'S IN THE FIGHT.
****

MORE PASSIONATE ABOUT HER PURPOSE
STRIVING TO ANSWER GOD'S CALL
THE DEBT SHE OWED; HE PAID IT ALL.
PRAYING AND TRUSTING BEING LED BY GOD'S HAND,
HE IS IN CONTROL,
HE HAS THE MASTER PLAN.
MORE HONEST ABOUT HER FAULTS SHE ADMITS WHEN
SHE'S WRONG,
IN HER WEAKEST HOURS
THE HOLY SPRIT MAKES HER STRONG.
IN CHRIST SHE ABIDES
NOT HAUGHTY, CONDENSINDING OR LIFTED IN PRIDE.
****

MORE IN TUNE TO HER HEALTH
STAYING FIT LIKE SHE SHOULD,
NOT SO HEAVENLY BOUND THAT SHE'S NO
EARTHLY GOOD.
****

MORE LOVE, PEACE AND BLESSING
THE LORD HAS IN STORE,
YOUR QUALITIES INCREASE,
THEY'RE HARD TO IGNORE.
WE LOVE YOU PASTOR JACKIE,
YOU ARE THE APPLE OF GOD'S EYE
THE GIFTS HE'S GIVEN YOU
ARE MORE THAN ANY ONE COULD BUY!!

MOTHER EARLENE'S BIRTHDAY

MY OH MY HOW YEARS DID FLY
PRECIOUS MEMORIES OF DAYS GONE BY.
SKIPPING DOWN THE GRADE SCHOOL HALL
NO CARES OR WORRIES NO - NONE AT ALL.
HOME FILLED WITH GIRLS AND BOYS
HAVING FUN WITH HOMEMADE TOYS
EACH SUNDAY WE MARCHED OFF TO CHURCH
BLEACHED WHITE BLOUSES,
STARCHED STIFF SKIRTS
ON EASTER I SAID MY SPEECH,
AT NIGHT; I LAY ME DOWN TO SLEEP.

LIVING MY DREAM
OF SWEET SIXTEEN,
THE PIGTAILS HAD TO GO,
WANTED TO WEAR MY BIG AFRO.
BLACK AND WHITE SADDLE SHOES,
WIDE BELL BOTTOMS, BOBBY SOX TOO.
THE HIGH SCHOOL PROM IT WAS NEXT
ONLY IF I PASSED THE HISTORY TEST.
COULDN'T WAIT TO GET A
POODLE SKIRT AND
HIGH HEEL SHOES, BOY HOW THEY HURT!
GRADUATION CAME AT LAST
SHOUTS OF JOY FROM ALL WHO PASSED.

COMING OF AGE ALMOST GROWN,
COULDN'T WAIT TO BE ON MY OWN.
GAVE THAT GUY A SPECIAL SMILE,
NOW WE'RE HEADED DOWN THE ISLE.
CHILDREN COMING ONE BY ONE,
THREE DAUGHTERS AND A SON.
LEARNED TO CUT HAIR, AND TWIST SOME CURLS,
BUT I WOULDN'T TRADE THEM FOR THE WORLD.
FAMILY CHORES WERE NEVER DONE,
CLEANING AND COOKING FROM SUN TO SUN.

I'M NOT LIVING IN THE PAST,
JUST AMAZED AT HOW
THE YEARS WENT SO FAST.
YES, THIS WORLD HAS SURELY CHANGED,
BUT MY FAITH IN GOD STILL REMAINS.

I'VE MOVED TO DIFFERENT PLACES,
MADE NEW FRIEND, SEEN DIFFERENT FACES.
I HAVE YEARS AND YEARS TO BE THANKFUL FOR
WHEN ONE DOOR CLOSED,
GOD OPENED MORE.
WITH HIS STRENGTH I'VE DONE MY BEST
KIDS ALL GROWN, NOW AN EMPTY NEST.

AS I SIT ON THE MOTHER'S BOARD
I SOMETIMES SMILE,
THINKING BACK WHEN I WAS A CHILD.
GONE ARE THE DAYS OF WHITE UNIFORMS

AND THICK COTTON HOSE.
COULDN'T WEAR LIPSTICK;
OR POWDER THEIR NOSE.
THE HYMNS THEY SANG
HELPED US TO RUN THIS RACE,
WE'VE COME THIS FAR SURELY BY FAITH.
WHAT A FRIEND WE HAVE IN JESUS
HOW I GOT OVER, THIS LITTLE LIGHT OF MINE,
I'M GONNA LET IT SHINE.

THE MOTHERS OF ZION
SALUTE YOU - 70 GOLDEN YEARS!
THERE'S BEEN SOME LAUGHTER,
SOMETIME TEARS.
THANK YOU LORD FOR OUR HEALTH AND STRENGTH
USE OF OUR ARMS AND HANDS
LEGS TO WALK ON WHEN WE STAND.
OUR MIND IS FIXED; OUR HEARTS ARE PURE
DON'T ASK ABOUT THE HAIR
ONLY CLAIROL KNOWS FOR SURE. :=))

OUR MOTHER HAYS

UNIQUE IN HER OWN WAY,
SHE LAYS DOWN THE LAW
AND BOY SHE DON'T PLAY.

FIRST TO ARRIVE ON SUNDAY MORNING......
ALL COMFY IN HER SEAT.
IF YOU'RE WEARING THEM DRESSES TO SHORT,
GET READY TO FACE THE HEAT.

BECAREUL WHAT YOU WEAR
AND WATCH HOW YOU DRESS
PASS DOWN THE LAP CLOTH
CAUSE SHE DON'T TAKE NO MESS.

MONTHLY COMMUNION
SHE GIVES ASSIGNMENTS
AND CHORES,
A MOTHERS ON THE
THE EAST AND THE WEST DOOR.
WORKING IN THE PANTRY,
PACKING BAGS READY TO GIVE
LEADING OTHERS TO CHRIST,
AND TEACHING THEM TO HOW TO LIVE.
GUIDING AND INSTRUCTING,
CALLING ON ALL THE MEN,
BRO WILLIE BETTER GET IT RIGHT
OR START OVER AGAIN.

AN AIDE TO PASTOR DEBORAH
SHE LOOKS OUT OVER THE FLOCK
EYES GOING TWO AND FRO,
NOTHING GETS BY HER
YOU BET SHE'LL LET YOU KNOW.

ON A MORE SERIOUS NOTE:
MOTHER HAYS PRAYERS ARE DEEP
STRAIGHT FROM THE SOUL,
A BEAUTIFUL SMILE AND A HEART AS PURE AS GOLD.

GOD HAD BLESSED YOU MOTHER HAYS WITH EIGHTY
LONG YEARS,
YOU'VE HAD SOME HEART ACHE, PAIN AND TEARS.

GOD HAS PRESERVED YOU
STILL STANDING STRONG,
YOU'VE KEPT THE FAITH
AND YOU'RE YET HOLDING ON.

WE LOVE YOU MO. HAYS
WHAT MORE CAN I SAY,
GRACEFUL YET FIRM
IN YOUR OWN WAY.
WE'LL HOLD YOUR HAND,
WE'VE GOT YOUR BACK,
BUT MO. HAYS WON'T YOU
PLEASE CUT US A LITTLE SLACK.

ENCOURAGEMENT

A LADY

WHAT IS THAT AWFUL SOUND,
THAT RINGING IN MY EAR?
I TOOK THE PILLOW OFF MY HEAD,
AND I HEARD IT LOUD AND CLEAR.

I SNATCHED IT OFF THE HOOK,
GAVE A SLEEPY
HELLO.................
"GOOD MORING!! A LIVELY REPLY!"
A VOICE I DID NOT KNOW.

"MY INVITATION IS STILL OPEN,"
SHE CONTINUED TO SAY,
"WAKE-UP RISE AND SHINE,
TODAY'S THE LORD'S DAY!"

NOT SUNDAY, I THOUGHT TO MYSELF,
IRRITATED AS I LOOKED AT THE TIME.
UP THIS EARLY ON SUNDAY,
SHE MUST BE OUTTA HER MIND!
ON SUNDAYS, I SLEEP IN,
I NEED THE EXTRA REST,
I PARTIED ALL NIGHT LONG,
NOW THAT I DO, MY BEST.

I STUDDERED AS I SPOKE,
"I, I, HAVE NOTHING TO WEAR.
NOT ONLY THAT,
YOU SHOULD SEE MY HAIR!"

"WHO IS THIS CALLING SO EARLY?"
"I DON'T REMEMBER YOU,
I TRIED TO CATCH YOUR VOICE,
BUT I DON'T HAVE A CLUE."

"YOU SAID YOU MET ME AT WORK,
WHEN I HAD A LOT ON MY MIND."
"WHAT DAY COULD THAT HAVE BEEN?"
"IT HAPPENS ALL THE TIME."

"OKAY…….PICK ME UP IN AN HOUR,
IF YOU WANT TO WAIT."
SHE WON'T ASK ME AGAIN,
AFTER WE GET THERE LATE.

SHE'LL TURN UP HER NOSE,
YOU KNOW THAT'S HOW CHURCH FOLKS DO.
WHEN YOU DON'T DRESS LIKE THEM,
THEIR TRUE COLORS COME THROUGH.

SHE'LL RUSH THROUGH THE DOOR,
PRETENDING I'M NOT HER GUEST,
LOOKING STRAIGHT AHEAD,
WHILE OTHERS LOOK AT MY DRESS.

"I WEAR WHAT I GOT!!
YOU INVITED ME,
TO PUT ME ON DISPLAY,
FOR THE WHOLE WORLD TO SEE."

IF THAT DOESN'T WORK,
I'LL JUST TELL IT ALL.
SHE'LL HATE THE DAY SHE PICKED ME UP,
OR EVER MADE THAT CALL.

WHAT I HAVE TO SAY,
WILL MAKE HER DROP HER HEAD.
I'LL TELL HER OF THAT STRANGER,
THAT JUST LEFT MY BED.

"HE HELPS ME FEED THE KIDS,
NOW WHAT DO YOU EXPECT ME TO DO?"
"MY BABY NEEDS NEW SHOES,
AND MY HELP AIN'T COMING FROM YOU!"

MUCH TO MY SURPRISE,
SHE WAS DIFFERENT,
I COULD TELL.
SHE DIDN'T CONDEMN ME WITH WORDS,
OR SEND ME STRAIGHT TO HELL.

SHE GAVE ME A FRIENDLY HUG,
A GLOW WAS IN HER EYES.
SHE DIDN'T STARE AT MY DRESS,
THAT WASN'T EVEN MY SIZE.

SHE TOLD ME OF <u>A LADY</u>,
THAT HAD BEEN MUCH LIKE ME.
HOW GOD HAD CHANGED HER LIFE,
HOW HE HAD SET HER FREE.

HER KIDS HAD BEEN HUNGRY,
AND SHE HAD RENT TO PAY.
SHE COUNTED ON THE MEN,
TO HELP ALONG THE WAY.

SHE TOLD ME THAT HER LIFE,
HAD BEEN AN AWFUL MESS.
SHE TRIED TO LIVE RIGHT,
BUT COULD NOT PASS THE TEST.

AT LAST SHE SURRENDERED TO JESUS,
THERE WAS NOTHING LEFT TO DO.
THE MEN HAD WALKED AWAY,
BUT JESUS CARRIED HER THROUGH.
EVERY DAY WASN'T SUNNY,
AND EVERYTHING WASN'T ON TRACT.
GOD WAS ON HER SIDE,
SHE KNEW HE HAD HER BACK.

I LISTENED VERY INTENTLY,
TO WHAT SHE HAD TO SAY.
THE TEARS FILLED MY EYES,
AS WE DROVE ALONG THE WAY.
WAS SHE THIS LADY,
OR WAS SHE TRYING TO RUN A GAME?

HOW COULD GOD CHANGE A LIFE,
GIVE HER A BRAND NEW NAME?

I SAT THROUGH THE SERVICE,
LISTENED TO EVERY WORD.
HOW GOD GAVE HIS SON,
WAS SOMETHING I HAD NEVER HEARD.

I RAN TO THE ALTER,
FELL ON MY KNEES,
CRIED OUT TO GOD,
LORD HELP ME, PLEASE!

I FELT THE LOVE OF JESUS,
JUST LIKE THE LADY SAID.
HIS LOVE FILLED MY HEART,
NOT JUST MY HEAD.
IF YOU'RE LIKE THAT LADY,
HE WILL DO THE SAME FOR YOU.
HE IS NO RESPECTOR OF PERSONS,
HIS LOVE IS REALLY TRUE.

NOW I'VE GOT TO MAKE A CALL,
LIKE THE ONE THAT WAS MADE TO ME.
TELL SOMEONE ABOUT A LADY,
THAT GOD HAS SET FREE!!

A LOST FRIEND

I GRIEVE AND CRY OVER THE LOSS OF A FRIEND
I SEARCH MY HEART DEEP WITHIN.

GRADE SCHOOL,
HIGH SCHOOL,
WE SHARED SO MUCH FUN,
WE GREW OLDER AND PARTED,
YOU KNOW LIFE ON THE RUN.....

WE MADE PROMISES
WE CROSSED OUR HEART
VOWED FROM CHILDHOOD
NEVER TO PART.

BUT THERE WAS NO TIME TO CHAT
WHEN I MET HER
ON THE STREET,
HAD TO HURRY HOME,
GET THESE SHOES OFF MY FEET.

I SENSED SOMETHING WAS WRONG,
BUT I COULDN'T MEET HER NEEDS,
I HAD MY OWN PROBLEMS
AND A FAMILY TO FEED.

WHAT HAD HAPPENED,
WHERE WAS HER SMILE,
WHERE WAS HER GLOW?
THE MARKS ON HER ARMS,
THEY LET ME KNOW.

I SAW IN HER EYES
HER HURT AND DESPAIR,
HER UNKEPT APPEARANCE,
AND UNCOMBED HAIR.

I SHOOK MY HEAD,
AND IN A DISCRETE WAY,
PASSED HER A DOLLAR, THEN RUSHED ON MY WAY.

SHE HAD THREE CHILDREN,
AND THAT WAS SO SAD,
HER HUSBAND WALKED OUT; NOW THEY HAD NO DAD.

I DIDN'T SHARE JESUS,
I KNEW HE WAS THE KEY,
I KNEW HE LOVED HER,
AS MUCH AS HE LOVED ME.

THEY FOUND HER ON THE STREET
THAT I PASS EVERYDAY.
THREE BEAUTIFUL CHILDREN NOW
TAKEN AWAY.

NOW I THINK BACK,
MY HEART SO SAD,
GRIEVING AND CRYING
OVER THE FRIEND I HAD.
IF I HAD STOPPED AND PRAYED
WHEN THERE WAS STILL TIME,
I WOULDN'T BE MOURNING WITH GUILT ON MY MIND.

GOD FORGIVE ME,
I DIDN'T ANSWER THE CALL,
WHAT WOULD IT HAVE COST ME? YOU PAID IT ALL.

IF I COULD TELL HER
I LOVE HER
HOW JOYFUL IT WOULD BE
BY THE GRACE OF GOD
IT COULD HAVE BEEN
ME.

WE PASS BY PEOPLE EVERYDAY.
OUR NOSE IN THE AIR,
NEW SET OF NAILS,
FRESHLY DONE HAIR.

WE THINK NO ONE IS WATCHING,
BUT JESUS CAN SEE.
HE SAID –
"IF YOU'VE DONE IT TO THEM,
YOU'VE DONE IT TO ME."

IF YOU'VE GOT A FRIEND
THAT WAS MUCH LIKE MINE,
STOP AND GIVE THEM SOME OF YOUR TIME.
IT WOULD ONLY TAKE A MINUTE,
TO HUG THEM AND PRAY,
A LIFE MAY BE SAVED AS
YOU GO YOUR WAY.

EACH DAY AS I KNEEL,
FATHER – I PRAY
ALLOW ME TO SHARE
YOUR LOVE TODAY.

TO REACH OUT AND TOUCH A HURTING SOUL
THEY'RE WORTH MORE
THAN DIAMONDS,
SILVER OR GOLD

I PRAY WHEN HEAVEN'S GATES
SWING OPEN AND I
WALK IN,
I'LL BE GREETED BY JESUS,
AND EVERY LONG LOST FRIEND.

A MOTHER'S LOVE

SHE WAKES EARLY MORNINGS,
HER CHILDREN LAY SLEEPING
IN BED.
SHE STARED OUT THE DINGY WINDOW
AND THIS IS WHAT SHE SAID.

"LORD, YOU SEE OUR NEED,
AND ALL THESE MOUTHS
I HAVE TO FEED."
"I'VE TRIED SO HARD SO VERY LONG,
I JUST CAN'T MAKE IT ON MY OWN."

"THEY DON'T KNOW WHAT I'M GOING THROUGH AND
DON'T UNDERSTAND MY PRAYERS TO YOU."
QUESTIONS THEY ALWAYS ASK, "MAMA WHY?"
"DON'T WORRY MY CHILD
THE LORD WILL SUPPLY."

"I'M HUNGRY MAMA,
WHAT WILL WE EAT?"
THE CUPBOARD IS EMPTY
NO BREAD, NO MEAT.
SHE'LL ASK FOR AN ADVANCE ON HER PAY
TO FEED HER FAMILY ONE MORE DAY.

"CAN I GET A BRAND NEW DRESS?" "AT
 SCHOOL EACH DAY
 I LOOK A MESS."
"YOU KNOW MY SHOES DON'T FIT
 AT ALL."
"CAN WE GO SHOPPING AT THE MALL?"

"MAMA WHY YOU PRAY SO MUCH,
 ALWAYS ASKING FOR THE MASTER'S TOUCH?"
"MAMA YOU ALWAYS ON YOUR KNEES,
 PRAYING LORD HELP ME PLEASE!"

I'M WEARY AND TIRED
 FROM WORKING ALL DAY,
 RENT AND BILLS I HAVE TO PAY.
 MY PRECIOUS CHILDREN LAY ASLEEP,
 MY LOVE FOR THEM GOES VERY DEEP.

NO FATHER AT HOME,
 A RIVER OF TEARS SWELLS HER EYES, TRUSTING AND
 PRAYING THE LORD WILL PROVIDE.

"LORD, YOU REIGN AND YOU RULE,
 PROTECT MY CHILDREN EACH DAY AT SCHOOL.
 KEEP THE ENEMY AT BAY
 HELP THEM TO WALK IN A RIGHTEOUS WAY."

SHE STANDS IN THE QUIET OF HER ROOM,
 PRAYING, "LORD BLESS

THE FRUIT OF MY WOMB."
GOD BENDS HIS EARS
TO A MOTHER'S CRY,
HE BOTTLES THE TEARS THAT FALL FROM HER EYES.

YEARS HAVE GONE SO QUICKLY BY,
NOW WE KNOW AND WE UNDERSTAND WHY.
THE LORD TOOK CARE OF MAMA
HE KEPT HER STRONG,
SHE LIVED TO SEE HER CHILDREN GROWN.

PLEASE
GIVE MAMA HER FLOWERS WHILE SHE LIVES
FOR ALL HER SACRIFICE AND THE LOVE SHE GIVES.
IF MAMA HAS GONE ON TO GLORY
THANK GOD FOR ALL SHE DID FOR YOU,
GOD IS STILL ANSWERING MAMA'S PRAYERS TOO.

A MOTHER'S LOVE
THERE'S NOT MUCH MORE TO SAY,
WISHING ALL MOTHERS A HAPPY MOTHERS DAY!!

BLAMELESS

I HAD WAITED FOR THE RAIN TO CEASE BEFORE I
WALKED OUTSIDE. REFLECTIONS OF MY PASS MADE
TEARS FILL MY EYES.
I STOOD LOOKING OUT THE WINDOW, MEMORIES
RACING THROUGH MY MIND. HOW CAN I LET GO OF
YESTERDAY, LEAVE MY TROUBLED LIFE BEHIND.

I JOINED THE CHURCH AND REPENTED OF MY
SINS, VOWED TO RUN THE CHRISTIAN RACE FROM
BEGINNING TO THE END.
THE CHOIR CAME NEXT, HIS PRAISES I SANG HIGH.
FOR A WRETCH LIKE ME, GOD SENT HIS SON TO DIE.
PRISON MINISTRY FOLLOWED, THAT'S WHERE I
MIGHT HAVE BEEN. EACH DAY HIS MERCIES
HE GAVE ME A CHANCE AGAIN. THE ENEMY CAME
WITH EVERY TEST, I STRIVED TO LIVE RIGHT TRYING
TO DO MY BEST.

WHAT IF SOMEONE FINDS OUT AND EXPOSE HOW I
LIVED, WOULD MY CHRISTIAN FAMILY ACCEPT ME
AND WOULD THEY FORGIVE? SEEMS AS HOURS HAD
PASSED, I MOVED TOWARDS THE DOOR. THEN WITH A
CHANGE OF HEART, I FELL TO THE FLOOR.

I PRAYED AND ASK THE LORD TO GUIDE ME
WITH HIS HAND. THE LOVE OF GOD FORGIVES,
CONDEMENDATION COMES FROM MAN.

WAS SOMEONE IN THE ROOM OR WAS THE SPIRIT
LOUD AND CLEAR. THE ENEMY OF GUILT AND SHAME
HAD FILLED MY HEART WITH FEAR.

HEAR ME BROTHERS AND SISTERS; RUN THE RACE
GOD SET FOR YOU, LOOK FORWARD AND DON'T
LOOK BACK. YOU MIGHT FALL AND SLIP AND GIVE
INTO SATAN'S ATTACK.

GOD HAS DECLARED YOU INNOCENT. HE GAVE YOU A
NEW START. FORGET WHAT'S BEHIND AND PRESS ON
TOWARDS THE MARK. THE LOVE OF GOD HAS PAID
FOR ALL OF YESTERDAY, BY HIS BLOOD HE FOUND
YOU BLAMELESS AND BLAMELESS YOU WILL STAY!!!

EMPTYNESS

I TRIED TO FILL THE EMPTYNESS,
THAT WOULD NOT GO AWAY.
PARTIES DRUS, WORDLY THINGS,
THAT EMPTYNESS WOULD STAY.

I TRIED TO FILL THE EMPTYNESS,
TRIED TO UNDERSTAND,
WHY I WASN'T SATISFIED
WITH THE PLEASURES OF MAN.

I TRIED TO FILL THE EMPTYNESS,
BY MOVING FROM TOWN TO TOWN.
THE EMPTYNESS WOULDN'T GO AWAY,
IT JUST HUNG AROUND.

I TRIED TO FILL THE EMPTYNESS,
BY MAKING DIFFERENT FRIENDS.
I'D PICK ONE UP, PUT ONE DOWN,
WILL THE CYCLE EVER END?

I TRIED TO FILL THE EMPTYNESS,
BY SPENDING ALL I HAD,
ALL THE STUFF AND THINGS I BOUGHT,
NEVER MADE ME GLAD.

I TRIED TO FILL THE EMPTYNESS,
BY GETTING A NEW JOB.
SURELY THAT WOULD DO,
THAT EMPTYNESS JUST STUCK AROUND
JUST LIKE SUPER GLUE.

I TRIED TO FILL THE EMPTYNESS,
BY GETTING A BRAND NEW SPOUSE,
BOUGHT A BRAND NEW CAR,
THEN A BRAND NEW HOUSE.
ALL THESE THINGS
GAVE ME LOTS OF PRIDE,
BUT THEY COULDN'T FILL THE EMPTYNESS THAT
WAS WAY DOWN DEEP INSIDE.

I TRIED TO FILL THE EMPTYNESS,
DRESSING LIKE OTHERS DO,
KEEPING UP WITH THE JONES' JUST MADE ME
EMPTY TOO.

I TRIED TO FILL THE EMPTYNESS,
I BOUGHT A MORE EXPENSIVE DRESS.
BUT THAT EMPTYNESS WAS IN MY HEART,
AND STILL I LOOKED A MESS.

I TRIED TO FILL THE EMPTYNESS,
WENT TO A BRAND NEW CHURCH,
SAT ON A BRAND NEW PEW,
STILL THAT STUBBORN EMPTYNESS

CAME RIGHT ALONG WITH ME TOO.

PEOPLE, MONEY, DIAMONDS, OR GOLD,
NOTHING I TRIED COULD FILL MY EMPTY SOUL.
BROKEN AND WOUNDED LIKE A HELPLESS CHILD,
TIRED AND DISCOURAGED,
I'D GONE MY LAST MILE.

I CRIED OUT TO GOD,
HIS SPIRIT SPOKE TO ME.
"OH, MY PRECIOUS CHILD,
YOU'VE WASTED SO MUCH TIME,
TRYING TO DO THE WORK THAT'S ALWAYS BEEN
MINE. "YOU'VE WAITED SO VERY LONG,
ONLY I CAN FILL THAT EMPTYNESS AND GIVE YOUR
HEART A SONG."

THE MESSAGE I LEAVE WITH YOU,
IS STRAIGHT FROM MY HEART.
TRUST AND DEPEND ON GOD,
WHEN YOUR WORLD SEEMS TORN APART.

DON'T DWELL ON THE EMPTYNESS,
TRYING TO MAKE IT GO AWAY.
WHERE THE WORD OF GOD IS PLANTED,
EMPTYNESS CAN'T STAY.

YOU ARE AN AWESOME CREATION
BE THANKFUL FOR THE

GIFTS WITHIN
HOLD YOU HEAD UP HIGH
DON'T LET EMPTYNESS WIN.

CAST ALL YOUR CARE ON CHRIST,
BECAUSE HE CARES FOR YOU,
HE WILL FILL THAT EMPTY SPACE,
THERE'S NOTHING THAT GOD CAN'T DO!!

FREE AT LAST

I PICTURE MYSELF AS A BIRD
HATCHED WAY UP HIGH.
I SEE CLOUDS, RAINBOWS
AND A BEAUTIFUL BLUE SKY.

I WANT TO SOAR LIKE AN EAGLE,
BUT MY FOOT IS CAUGHT IN A LIMB.
HOPES OF ME FLYING IS LOOKING PRETTY DIM.

WHAT HAS ME BOUND,
I LOOK AROUND TO SEE
A LIMB OF MY BLACKNESS KEEPS STARING
BACK AT ME.

I TRY TO FREE MYSELF FROM THE LIMB,
THE VISION SEEMS TO REPEAT.
THIS LIMB IS PULLING ME BACK,
IT'S HOLDING ONTO MY FEET.

MY PEOPLE BRING ME STRENGTH,
PEOPLE THAT ARE BLACK LIKE ME.
THERE ARE BATTLE SCARS AND INJURIES,
HOW DID THEY GET FREE?

DON'T FLY AWAY AND LEAVE ME,
TELL ME WHAT TO DO.

I SEE WOUNDS AND SCARS
THAT COULD HAVE KILLED YOU.
TELL ME
HOW DID YOU SURVIVE?

WISDOM SPOKE,
AND I LISTENED CLOSE,
AND THIS WAS THEIR REPLY.

"STRONG BLACK SOLDIERS
MARCHED ON BEFORE,
BREAKING DOWN BARRIERS AND EVERY
CLOSED DOOR."

"HARRIET TUBMAN, FREDERICK DOUGLAS,
MARCUS GARVEY
ONLY TO NAME A FEW."
"THEY WERE TRAIL BLAZERS
THAT PAVED THE WAY
FOR SISTERS AND BROTHERS
LIKE ME AND YOU."

SOME BATTLES MAY TAKE YOU DOWN,
DON'T GIVE UP THE FIGHT
AT THE END OF EVERY TUNNEL,
THERE IS A BEAM OF LIGHT!

THAT LIMB WAS IN MY MIND
AND NOT REAL AT ALL,

IT WAS THE FEAR OF ME SOARING,
AFRAID THAT I MIGHT FALL.

LOOK AROUND YOUR FEET
SEE WHAT'S HOLDING YOU:
LIMBS OF REJECTION,
LIMBS OF BROKEN DREAMS,
LIMBS OF DISAPPOINTMENT,
THE LIST COULD GO ON AND ON.
TAKE THE STRENGTH FROM
YOUR PEOPLE
PASS IT TO YOUR DAUGHTERS
AND SONS.

MY PRAYER FOR YOU

I PRAY THE LORD WILL BLESS YOU,
AND MEND YOUR BROKEN HEART.
THE ANGELS WILL WIPE YOUR TEARS AND
GOD HEALS WHAT'S TORN APART.

I PRAY HE GIVES YOU STRENGTH,
WHEN YOU'RE IN YOUR WEAKEST HOUR,
YOU CAN MAKE IT ANOTHER DAY
BY HIS MERCY AND HIS POWER.

I PRAY YOU KNOW HE'S WITH YOU
WHEN THERE'S SO MUCH DARKNESS AND GLOOM,
I PRAY HE SENDS RAYS OF SUNSHINE
TO BRIGHTEN UP YOUR ROOM.

I PRAY YOU KEEP ON MOVING
IN SPITE OF THE MOUNTAINS YOU FACE TODAY,
SPEAK TO THOSE GIANT MOUNTAINS,
AND THEY WILL GET OUTTA YOUR WAY.

I PRAY GOD GIVES YOU PEACE
WHEN FACING THE TRIALS OF LIFE
AND PUT TO GRUELING TESTS
I PRAY EVERY MORNING YOU RISE
AND SAY
TODAY I'LL DO MY BEST!

I KNOW THAT YOU'VE BEEN WOUNDED
THE QUESTION YOU ASK
IS WHY?
THE PAIN SO UNBEARABLE,
BUT YOU CAN MAKE IT IF YOU TRY!
DON'T SAY THAT I DON'T KNOW –
OH YES, I'VE BEEN THERE TOO.
THAT'S WHY I CAN TELL YOU
JUST WHAT GOD CAN DO.

YOU WILL WANT SOMEONE TO TALK TO
WHEN YOU'RE DOWN AND ALL ALONE,
THE PLANS YOU HAD FOR THE FUTURE,
DESTROYED
ALL HOPE IS GONE.

TODAY I'M PRAYING FOR YOU,
I LIFT YOUR NAME TO GOD ABOVE
AND WHEN YOU FACE TOMORROW,
YOU FEEL THE PRESENCE OF HIS LOVE.
REMEMBER YOU MADE IT THE DAY BEFORE,
MY PRAYER IS FOR YOU TO LIVE,
AND SEE WHAT GOD HAS IN STORE.

I PUT MY TRUST IN GOD,
ON HIS WORD I STAND
TODAY I'M PRAYING FOR YOU
IN JESUS NAME AMEN!
DON'T GIVE UP,
DON'T GIVE UP.

REJOICE YOUR WAY THROUGH

WHEN THINGS GO WRONG, AND THEY
SOMETIMES WILL,
WHEN THE ROAD YOU'RE TRAVELING
SEEMS ALL UP HILL.
KEEP MOVING FORWARD,
DON'T LOOK BEHIND,
GOD WILL GIVE YOU STRENGTH TO CLIMB.
THE ENEMY WANTS TO FIGHT
AND PULL YOU BACK DOWN.
PRAISE...... IS YOUR WEAPON
NOW STAND YOUR GROUND!

WHEN YOU'VE LOST YOUR JOB,
AND THE RENT IS DUE,
THE KIDS ARE SICK
CAN'T SEE YOUR WAY THROUGH.
DRY YOUR EYES, AND LEND AN EAR,
GOD IS IN THE BATTLE; PLEASE DON'T
FEAR.
REJOICE IN THE LORD
WHILE YOU'RE IN THE FIGHT,
WEAPING ONLY ENDURES FOR A NIGHT.
THERE IS NOTHING TO HARD FOR GOD TO DO,
YOUR RENT WILL GET PAID
AND THE KIDS FED TOO.
REJOICE, REJOICE, REJOICE.

WHEN YOUR CUTOFF NOTICE CAME IN THE MAIL,
IN ALL YOUR TRYING, YOU SEEM TO FAIL.
GOD PROMISED HE WOULD SEE YOU THROUGH
PRAISE HIM, REJOICE, HIS WORD IS TRUE!
THE ENEMY THINKS HE'S DEFEATED YOU,
THINKS HE'S SO SMART,
IN YOUR DARKEST HOUR
IS WHEN YOUR PRAISES START.
AT MIDNIGHT
START TO SING AND PRAISE
THE SUN WILL SHINE
AND BRIGHTEN YOUR DAYS.

WHEN THE REFRIGERATOR IS EMPTY
AND YOUR WALLET IS TOO,
YOU'RE CRYING AND PRAYING
LORD WHAT DO I DO?
I READ THE WORD,
THIS IS WHAT IT SAID.
"THE RIGHTEOUS IS NOT FORSAKEN,
NOR HIS SEED BEGGING BREAD."
PRAISE THE LORD AND SEE
WHAT IT BRINGS;
NO WANT OR LACK FOR ANY GOOD THING.
REJOICE AND PRAISES GO HAND IN HAND
SEE HOW IT CANCELS THE ENEMY'S PLAN.

WHEN YOUR FAMILY SEEMS TO FALL APART
THE KIDS DO THINGS THAT BREAK YOUR HEART.

THE TRICK OF THE EMENY
IS TO PUT YOU TO A TEST.
YOU'VE FASTED AND PRAYED,
YOU'VE DONE YOUR BEST.
NOTHING SEEMS TO BE GOING YOUR WAY,
WHOSE BATTLE IS IT ANYWAY?
DANCE, SING, PRAISE WITH A SHOUT,
SEE HOW THE LORD WILL BRING YOU OUT!

WHEN THE DOCTOR SAYS
"I'VE DONE ALL I CAN."
DON'T TRUST OR RELY ON
THE WORD OF MAN.
YOUR HEALTH IS WHAT THE
ENEMY IS TRYING TO STEAL,
REMEMBER,
BY HIS STRIPES WE WERE HEALED.
PRAISE HIM EACH AND EVERYDAY,
WATCH THAT MOUNTAIN MOVE
OUTTA YOUR WAY.

TRIALS WILL COME,
BUT THEY WON'T LAST LONG;
PRAISE AND GIVE THE LORD A SONG.
FOCUS ON GOD,
HIS LOVE IS REAL
NO MATTER HOW IT LOOKS
OR HOW YOU FEEL.
DEFEAT THE ENEMY,

WHEN THE ENEMY TRIES TO ATTACK,
PRAISE WILL STOP HIM DEAD
RIGHT IN HIS TRACKS!
MARCH LIKE JOSHUA
AROUND AND AROUND
SOUND A SHOUT OF PRAISE
AND WATCH THE ENEMY FALL DOWN.
LET THE LORD HEAR YOU RAISE YOUR VOICE,
REJOICE, REJOICE, REJOICE!!

THE PROVIDENCE OF GOD

I BRUSHED BACK THE TEARS
BECAUSE MY SHELVES WERE BARE.
I LOOKED IN ON MY CHILDREN
I PRAYED; "LORD KEEP THEM IN YOUR CARE."

HOW WILL I FEED THEM
THE WORRY TRIED TO CAPTURE MY MIND.
I KNOW HOW FAR HE'S BROUGHT ME AND
I PUT THOSE FEARS BEHIND.

THE PROVIDENCE OF GOD
HAS CARRIED ME DAY BY DAY
HIS WORD SAYS NOT TO FRET
ONLY TRUST AND OBEY.

I FELL ON MY KNEES
MY PRAYERS WERE NOT IN VAIN.
I PUT MY TRUST IN THE LORD
I PRAYED IN JESUS NAME.

GOD IS NOT A MAN THAT HE SHOULD LIE
PHILLIPANS 4:19
SAYS ALL MY NEEDS HE WOULD SUPPLY.

I CAN'T WAIT UNTIL THE BATTLE IS OVER
I HAVE TO SHOUT NOW

HE MADE A WAY BEFORE
AND HE WILL DO IT AGAIN SOME HOW!

GOD WILL DO JUST WHAT HE SAID AND THAT I
HAVE NO DOUBT
PRAISES ON MY LIPS
AS I RAN THROUGH THE HOUSE.

I KNEW I COULDN'T QUIT
I COULDN'T GIVE UP THE FIGHT.
THE HOLY SPIRIT ASSURED ME THAT THINGS WILL
BE ALRIGHT.

THE PROVIDENCE OF GOD
HE HAS MAPPED OUT MY LIFE,
HE DID NOT BRING ME THIS FAR TO LEAVE ME
I WALK BY FAITH AND NOT BY SIGHT.

THE PHONE RANG
AND IT STARTLED ME!
I HAD BEEN MEDITATING ON GOD'S WORD
THE SOUND OF A FAMILIAR VOICE
THIS IS WHAT I HEARD.

"THE CHURCH HAS A FOOD BASKET BEING
DELIVERED TO YOU."
MY PRAYERS HAS BEEN ANSWERED
GOD CAME THROUGH!

"OH BY THE WAY,
THE JOB YOU APPLIED FOR
IS ALSO YOURS TODAY."

HE PROVIDED HOUSING, FOOD
AND CLOTHES TO WEAR,
HE FILLED MY BARNS WITH PLENTY
ENOUGH FOR ME TO SHARE.

AS THE NEW YEAR APPROACHES
HIS GRACE
WILL TAKE YOU HIGHER
THE PROVIDENCE OF GOD
HE IS JEHOVAH-JIREH!!

WHOM THE SON SETS FREE IS FREE

MY HOMIES WOULD WHISPER,
MAN................,
MAKE YOU SOME BREAD.
IT'S LIKE TAKING CANDY
FROM A BABY
THAT'S WHAT THEY SAID.
LURED TO THE STREETS,
THEN I COMMITTED THE CRIME.
LOOKING OUT THROUGH BARS,
NOW DOING HARD TIME.

I HEARD THE LOCK CLICK,
HANDS CUFFED BEHIND MY BACK.
HUNTED DOWN LIKE AN ANIMAL,
STOPPED DEAD IN ITS TRACK.
NOW CALLED BY A NUMBER,
STRIPPED OF MY NAME.
GAVE UP THE FUBU,
FOR UNIFORMS, THAT LOOKS THE SAME.

NOW I FOLLOW, A DAILY ROUTINE,
MOPING DIRTY FLOORS,
KEEPING THEM NICE AND CLEAN.
I OBEYED ALL THE RULES THE
BOSSMAN GAVE,
TREATED LIKE AN ANIMAL,
LOCKED IN A CAGE.

THE DRUGS SEEMED EASY,
I CAN STOP WHEN I PLEASE,
NOW THE PAIN OF <u>NOT</u> HAVING IT,
HAS BROUGHT ME TO MY KNEES.
THE MATERIAL THINGS LOOKED GOOD,
CARS, CLOTHES AND SHOES
SMOKE A LITTLE POT,
DRINK A LITTLE BOOZE.
RIDING AROUND IN MY
CADDIE,
WITH NOTHING BUT TIME,
THE DEVIL SAW ME COMING,
AND PUT THOUGHTS IN MY MIND.

THE STORE THAT I ROBBED,
TOOK THINGS THAT DIDN'T
BELONG TO ME,
PEOPLE I ATTACKED,
CAUSED THEM PAIN AND MISERY.
WHY DID I DO IT?
WHY WAS I LED ASTRAY?
WHAT YOU SEW IN LIFE,
YOU WILL HAVE TO PAY.

THAT TURF I WAS PROTECTING,
WHERE SOMEONE TOOK A HIT;
JUST CONCRETE STAINED WITH BLOOD
THAT MY FAMILY WOULDN'T GET.
WHO CARES ABOUT MY FAMILY?
WHO CARES ABOUT MY LIFE?
I STARE AT THE CEILING,

AS I LAY WAKE AT NIGHT.
I CAN HEAR INMATES CRYING,
AS I START PRAYING IN MY CELL,
STRIPPED OF HIS MANHOOD,
AND THEY DARED HIM NOT TO TELL.

THE BRAIN GOD GAVE ME,
WHAT WAS I USING IT FOR?
TO GO IN AND OUT OF PRISON,
THROUGH A REVOLVING DOOR?
THAT WASN'T SO HARD,
ANYONE CAN DO THAT.
BUT, GOD GAVE ME THIS HEAD
FOR MORE THAN JUST A HAT.

AS I LAY THERE THINKING,
I COULD HEAR MY GRANDMA'S VOICE,
"MAKE JESUS YOUR LORD,
AND YOU'VE MADE THE RIGHT CHOICE!"

I PICKED UP A BIBLE,
I READ FAST AS I COULD,
ONE VERSE SO CLEAR,
NOW I UNDERSTOOD.
IT SANK DEEP IN MY HEART,
YOU KNOW WHAT I MEAN.
THE THIRD BOOK OF JOHN
VERSE SIXTEEN.
"FOR GOD SO LOVED THE WORLD,
HE GAVE HIS ONLY SON."
HE PAID A PRICE FOR

SOMETHING I HAD DONE.

EARLY ONE MORNING,
I GOT DOWN ON MY KNEES.
I SAID A SIMPLE PRAYER,
"LORD HELP ME PLEASE!"
THE PEACE OF GOD FILLED
MY CELL
YES I WAS DIFFERENT,
AND EVERYONE COULD TELL.

I MADE A PROMISE TO GOD,
IF HE WOULD SET ME FREE
I WOULD TELL THE WORLD
JUST WHAT HE DID FOR ME.
GOD'S WORD IS TRUE,
HE TURNED MY LIFE AROUND.
I'VE TAKEN A NEW ROAD,
THAT'S NOT PRISON BOUND.

IT WASN'T EASY,
AND I WAS PUT TO THE TEST,
THE WORK WAS HARD,
BUT, I DID MY BEST.
I WAS MADE IN GOD'S IMAGE
AND HE GAVE ME DOMINION TOO.
A CAGE IS FOR AN ANIMAL,
NOT FOR ME OR YOU.

NOW I GO BACK TO THE PRISON
BUT NOT TO STAY,

TO TELL LOST SOULS,
WHAT GOD HAS TO SAY.
GOD GAVE US A PROMISE,
AND HIS WORD WON'T FAIL.
HE WILL SET YOU FREE,
WHILE YOU'RE STILL LOCKED IN JAIL.

HE WILL GIVE YOU A NEW LIFE,
LEAVE THE OLD ONE BEHIND.
HE'LL GIVE FREEDOM TO YOUR SOUL,
FREEDOM TO YOUR MIND.
BE HONEST WITH GOD,
MEAN IT FROM YOUR HEART,
HE'LL FORGIVE YOUR SINS,
GIVE YOU A NEW START.

DON'T SIT BEHIND THOSE BARS
WAITING TO HIT THE STREET AGAIN
TO HOOK UP WITH YOUR HOMIES,
YOUR SO CALLED FRIENDS.
DON'T GIVE INTO THE SYSTEM
YOU'RE BETTER THAN THAT
USE THAT HEAD FOR MORE
THAN JUST A HAT.

GOD HAS YOUR ANSWER,
HE HOLDS THE KEY
SURRENDER TO HIS CALL
ONLY THEN WILL YOU BE FREE!!

YOUR BODY BELONGS TO THE LORD

A STRANGER STOPPED BY TODAY,
INTRODUCED AS MOM'S NEW FRIEND.
HE SMILED AS HE SHOOK MY HAND,
I EXAMINED HIM AS HE WALKED IN.

BRIGHT SHINNY SHOES,
DRESSED REAL NICE AND NEAT.
MADE HIMSELF AT HOME,
PICKED OUT HIS FAVORITE SEAT.

"WHEN IS HE LEAVING?" I ASK,
"IS HE GOING SOON?"
"BE QUIET!" WAS HER ANSWER,
"NOW GO BACK TO YOUR ROOM!"

MOM SEEMED SO HAPPY,
SHE HAD FOUND A REAL FRIEND.
SHE SAID,
"THINGS WILL BE MUCH BETTER,
THE DAY THAT HE MOVES IN."

I COULDN'T GO TO HER ROOM,
WITHOUT KNOCKING ON THE DOOR.
THE NIGHTS HE CAME HOME LATE,
SHE PACED AND WALKED THE FLOOR.

I MISSED THE TIMES I SPENT WITH HER,
OUR QUIET EVENINGS ALONE.
THE SECRETS WE SHARED AND LAUGHED ABOUT,
WERE MEMORIES,
THE GOOD TIMES GONE.

SOMETIMES I HEARD THEM FIGHTING,
I HEARD EVERY WORD THEY SAID.
WHEN MOM WENT TO WORK,
AND HE STAYED HOME IN BED.

THE BEGINNING OF THE END,
IT CAME TO PASS ONE DAY.
NOW I'M TELLING IT TO MY COUNSELOR,
THIS IS WHAT I HADTO SAY.

"COME INTO THE BEDROOM," HE SAID,
"LOOK AT MY NEW CAP."
"YOUR MOM HAS GONE TO WORK,
 SO SIT DOWN ON MY LAP."

"IF YOU TELL OUR LITTLE SECRET,
 I'LL PACK UP AND MOVE AWAY,"
YOUR MOM WILL BE SO SAD,
 SHE WON'T BELIEVE A WORD YOU SAY."

I DIDN'T LIKE BEING AT HOME,
I FELT REAL SICK INSIDE.
I WANTED TO BE PURE,

UNTIL I BECAME A BRIDE.

EACH DAY I WAS TORMENTED,
I CRIED, AND I WOULD PRAY.
"LORD, MAKE HIM LEAVE,
MAKE HIM GO AWAY."

THE SHAME AND GUILT I FELT,
SADNESS FILLED MY HEART.
NO HOPE FOR THE FUTURE,
MY DREAMS TORN APART.

SHOULD I SAY MORE?
OR DO YOU REALLY MIND?
THE DETAILS PRETTY GORY,
SO READ BETWEEN THE LINES.

I PRAYED TO THE LORD,
"PLEASE GIVE ME THE STRENGTH TO TELL."
I WAS AN AWFUL WRECK,
MY GRADES AT SCHOOL HAD FELL.

THE DAY FINALLY CAME,
I COULD TAKE NO MORE.
I TOOK A LONG DEEP BREATH,
AND WALKED THROUGH MY COUNSELORS DOOR.

GOD'S LOVE HEALED ME.
I PUT THE PAST BEHIND,

HE GAVE ME THIS PRECIOUS BODY, AND PEACE
TO MY MIND.

I KNOW THAT I'M A JEWEL,
THE APPLE OF GOD'S EYE.
THE DEVIL HAD ME FOOLED,
HE TOLD ME, LIE AFTER LIE.

GOD GAVE ME NEW HOPE, AND HE GAVE ME
NEW DREAMS.
YOUR BODY BELONGS TO THE LORD,
1ST CORINTHIANS 6:19.

WHAT GOD CAN DO

I BELIEVED IN MY HEART;
THE DIVORCE WAS RIGHT;
I WAS TIRED OF THE STRUGGLE
I GAVE UP THE FIGHT.

I HAD NAGGED AND COMPLAINED,
HIS FAULT WAS ALL I COULD SEE.
WHEN I MOVED OUT,
NO ONE WAS THERE FOR ME.

I WAS HIDING MY FEELINGS,
TRYING TO PRETEND,
ALL WAS FINE
BEING ALONE AGAIN.

HE NEVER HIT ME AND
HE DIDN'T FIGHT,
IF I HAD GIVEN IT TO GOD
HE WOULD HAVE MADE IT ALL RIGHT.

I HAD PRAYED FOR MY SPOUSE
TO CHANGE,
CONFORM TO WHAT I WANTED HIM
TO BE
AND DIDN'T REALIZE
THE CHANGE NEEDED WAS IN ME.

I WOULD PONDER OVER THE FACT
PEOPLE ARE DIFFERENT,
NO TWO ARE THE SAME,
GOD MADE US THAT WAY
HE CALLED US EACH BY NAME.

THERE SEEMED TO BE NO SUNSHINE,
ONLY RAIN,
HEARTACHE, DISPAIR
AND UNBEARABLE PAIN.

I WAITED AND WAITED
AS THE YEARS PASSED BY,
GOD MADE ME A PROMISE,
AND HE CANNOT LIE.

SOME MIRACLES TAKE TIME
WAS ALL I COULD HEAR,
NO MATTER HOW IT LOOKED,
OR HOW DEEP THE FEAR.

WHERE ARE YOU GOD?
I WAS PUT TO THE TEST.
I HAD MADE MY OWN
DECISIONS
THAT JUST WEREN'T THE BEST.

I MADE MISTAKES,
GOD,
FORGIVE ME PLEASE.
I STAYED IN GOD'S FACE,
AND DOWN ON MY KNEES.

THE WILDERNESS EXPERIENCE
IT WAS GOOD FOR ME,
GOD SHOWED ME THINGS
I HAD FAILED TO SEE.

MY LIFE WAS PREDESTINED
BEFORE THE WORD BEGAN,
HE HAD CARVED MY NAME IN THE PALM
OF HIS HAND.
FORGIVENESS IS THE PLACE TO START,
MAN LOOKS OUTWARD,
GOD SEES THE HEART.

I PACKED MY BAGS,
MOVED BACK HOME,
I THOUGHT I HAD THE VICTORY,
WHEN I LEFT HIM ALONE.

THANK GOD FOR HIS MERCY
AND HIS LOVE FOR ME.
HE OPENED MY EYES
NOW I CAN SEE.

NOW LET ME CONCLUDE WITH WHAT I WANT TO SAY
FOR SOMEONE WAITING ON GOD TODAY.

STAY WITH YOUR SPOUSE,
HE'S A GROWN MAN THAT'S TRUE,
TRYING TO CHANGE HIM
IS GOD'S WORK TO DO.

GOD CAME THROUGH FOR ME
HE WILL COME THROUGH FOR YOU,
TRUST AND DON'T DOUBT
HIS WORD IS SO TRUE!

FAMILY

MY PRECIOUS GIFTS

CHILDREN ARE A GIFT FROM THE LORD
THAT'S WHAT THE BIBLE SAYS,
I READ PSALM 127; IT'S IN MY HEART AND MY HEAD.

BRIAN, GAIL, AARON AND VERNON JR.
THE FOUR PRECIOUS GIFTS THE LORD GAVE TO ME,
HE MADE EACH ONE UNIQUE
THEIR DIFFERENCES IS PLAIN TO SEE.

<u>BRIAN,</u> THE OLDEST, OH WHAT A CUTE DELIGHT, BUT
HE HAD THE TIME MIXED UP,
CAUSE HE WOULDN'T SLEEP AT NIGHT.
BORN ON CHRISTMAS EVE,
HE COULDN'T UNDERSTAND WHY, ONLY ONE GIFT
WAS HIS YEARLY CRY!
HE FELT CHEATED, HE HAD TO SHARE HIS SPECIAL DAY,
BUT THERE WERE OTHER TOYS TO BUY AND MANY
BILLS TO PAY.
SOMETIME HIS GRADES AT SCHOOL WOULD FALL; I
WOULD ASK HIM WHY?
HE SAID, LUNCH WAS HIS FAVORITE SUBJECT AND
THEY DIDN'T MAKE NO APPLE PIE.
ROLLER SKATING AND SWIMMING WERE THINGS HE
ENJOYED THE MOST.

PANCAKES FOR BREAKFAST AND SOMETIME
FRENCH TOAST.
GROWING UP HE FLURISHED,
HE HAD MANY BRIGHT IDEAS,
THE DAY HE FELL IN LOVE, ENDED HIS NAVY CAREER.

GAIL, SHE CAME SECOND; MY GIFT FROM GOD
ABOVE, BORN TWO DAYS BEFORE MY BIRTHDAY, A
BUNDLE OF JOY TO LOVE.
SHE GREW QUICKLY AS SWEET AS SHE COULD
BE. WRAPPED HER FINGER AROUND YOUR HEART,
WHICH SHE HELD THE KEY.
GAIL (WE CALLED HER FUSSY GUSSIE) IF SHE WASN'T
DRY, AFTER THAT SHE WAS PLEASANT AND HARDLY
EVER CRIED.
ACTING AS HER BROTHER'S OTHER MOTHER, SHE
TOLD ALL THEY DID.
AT HOME, SCHOOL OR PLAY, NO SECRETS WERE HID.
GUSSIE WAS DIFFERENT, SHE WAS QUIET AND
OBSERVING, NOT LOUD, HER HUMBLE DEMEANOR
MADE HER STAND OUT IN A CROWD.
NO PARTYING, NO STAYING OUT LATE AT NIGHT,
SHE WAS VERY SERIOUS AND WANTED TO
MAKE IT RIGHT.
THANK GOD SHE WAS NO PROBLEM, SPECIAL IN
HER OWN WAY.
WE STILL CALL HER GUSSIE, AND FUSSY GUSSIE SHE
WILL STAY!

AARON, HE WAS THIRD, THE MIDDLE CHILD FOR ME,
ALWAYS LAUGHING
HAPPY AS COULD BE.
ARRON SOMETIMES GITTY AND SILLY, MY MOTHER
GAVE HIM A NAME,
(WACKY) WAS WHAT SHE CALLED HIM AND IT
STILL REMAINS.
AARON ADMIRED HIS BROTHER BRIAN; HE LAUGHED
AT EVERYTHING HE SAID AND DID,
IF THEY GOT INTO MISCHIEF, AARON KEPT IT HID.
HE ROLLER SKATED AND SWAM LIKE BRIAN, THEY
ENJOYED SO MUCH FUN. AARON WAS DIFFERENT;
REMEMBER HE WAS THE MIDDLE ONE.
AARON WAS A FRIENDLY CHILD; EVERYONE WAS HIS
FRIEND. HE WOULD LAUGH AND SMILE, AT WHAT
THEY SAID; THEY ALWAYS MADE HIM GRIN.
HE WAS SO KIND AND GIVING, SATAN TRIED TO PULL
HIM IN; AND LEAD TO DESTRUCTION DOWN THE
ROAD OF SIN. HE SAID PRAYERS KEPT HIM GOING
FULL SPEAD AHEAD, HE REMEMBERED THE PRAYERS
OF HIS GRANDMOTHER AND EVERY WORD SHE SAID.
AARON FINALLY ADMITTED HE COULDN'T KEEP UP
THE PACE. PRAISE GOD HE GAVE HIS LIFE TO JESUS
AND JOINED THE CHRISTIAN RACE!

VERNON, MY FOURTH, SWEET AS CHOCOLATE
CREAM PIE. I WAS OLDER AND MORE EXPERIENCED,
HE WAS THE APPLE OF MY EYE. QUIET NOT MUCH
TO SAY, HE HAD A FRIEND OR TWO. THE OLDER

SIBLINGS LOOKED AFTER HIM THEY THOUGHT THAT
WAS WHAT TO DO. GAIL, (GUSSIE) TREATED HIM LIKE
HER BABY, SHE WAS OLDER TOO YOU SEE, WHEN I
WASN'T AROUND, SHE TOOK THE PLACE OF ME.
VERNON LOVED FOOTBALL; HE WATCHED IT
WHENEVER HE COULD. ALL THE TALK AND ALL THE
GAME PLAYS, I NEVER UNDERSTOOD. MEAN JOE
GREENE AND TONY DORSETT, ONE TV IN THE HOUSE
WHERE THE FAMILY ALL SAT. SLOW AND EASY WAS
HIS WAY, COOL BREEZE THEY CALLED HIM AND
COOL BREEZE HE WOULD STAY.

MY GIFTS ALL GROWN AND ON THEIR OWN. I ASK
THE LORD TO BLESS AND KEEP THEM
AS THEY TRAVEL EACH DAY; HIS MERCY AND GRACE,
I STAND ON ALL THE WAY!
THE ROAD WE TRAVELED WAS NOT ALWAYS WELL;
BUT GOD GAVE ME THESE GIFTS AND HE CHOSE
THEM WELL!
THE SEED OF THE RIGHTEOUS WILL BE DELIVERED;
THAT'S WHAT THE BIBLE SAYS. CLEANSE MY HEART
AND MAKE ME RIGHT, KEEP MY GIFTS AND HOLD ON
TIGHT. THE WORD OF GOD IS VERY TRUE, SO WHEN
SOMEONE GIVES YOU A GIFT A WORD OF "THANKS"
IS WHAT TO DO!

THEY ALL HAVE THEIR FAMILIES NOW, I HAVE
GRANDCHILDREN GALORE. PLEASE DON'T ASK HOW
MANY, A SURPRISE ALWAYS INSTORE!!

THE PLAN OF GOD

A COUPLE MET YEARS AGO.
TEENAGERS.
THEY FELL IN LOVE,
THE DEVIL DIDN'T KNOW IT,
BUT THE PLAN WAS FROM GOD ABOVE.

THEY WORKED HARD AND GREW TOGETHER,
THEIR SMALL BEGINNINGS WERE
STEPPING STONES,
THE ENEMY HAD A PLAN
AND WOULD NOT LEAVE THEM ALONE.

THEIR ROAD WASN'T EASY,
BUT THEY VOWED TO STICK IT OUT.
OBSTACLES IN THEIR WAY,
THEY HAD FAITH
AND DIDN'T DOUBT.

THE YEARS PASSED QUICKLY,
THERE WERE STORMS AND THERE WERE TRIALS.
BUT THEY MARCHED ON AHEAD,
THEY WENT THAT EXTRA MILE.

THEY STARTED AN AWESOME MINISTRY
LOST SOULS WERE COMING IN.

RECEIVING CHRIST IN THEIR HEART AND BEING
SAVED FROM SIN.
THEY TOILED BOTH DAY AND NIGHT,
NOW THE BATTLE HAD BEGUN,
THE DEVIL AND HIS IMPS
AGAINST THE FATHER AND THE SON.

THIS COUPLE DIDN'T KNOW IT,
BUT, THE FOCUS WAS NOT ON THEM,
THE ENEMY PLAYED WITH THEIR MINDS, AND
THINGS WERE LOOKING PRETTY GRIM.

A BLOW FROM THE ENEMY KNOCKED THEM DOWN,
THEY CRIED OUT TO GOD,
SEEMS HE SIMPLY COULDN'T BE FOUND.

GOD'S WAYS ARE NOT LIKE OURS
AND TIME IS IN HIS HANDS;
HIS PLAN WON'T BE ABORTED
NO MATTER HOW IT LOOKS
TO MAN.

THEY PUT THEIR TRUST IN GOD WHEN THINGS
WEREN'T GOING RIGHT,
THE BATTLES AND WARS WERE WON,
IN WHICH THEY DID NOT HAVE TO FIGHT.
GOD SENT WARING ANGLES
STOPPED THE DEVIL IN HIS TRACKS
EVERYTHING HE STOLE,

HE HAD TO GIVE IT BACK.

WHAT GOD HAS JOINED TOGETHER
NO DEVIL CAN TEAR APART
GOD IS IN CONTROL,
HE KNEW THE END BEFORE THE START.

WE CAME TO WITNESS THE MARRIAGE OF A COUPLE,
THAT'S STILL VERY MUCH IN LOVE,
AND TO SERVE NOTICE ON THE DEVIL,
THIS PLAN WAS FROM GOD ABOVE.

A GROWN MAN CRY

HE PULLED INTO THE DRIVEWAY,
WALKED IN AND CLOSED THE DOOR,
NOW HE COULD LET HIS GUARD DOWN,
ALONE AGAIN ONCE MORE.

HE WALKED INTO THE KITCHEN,
FIXED A NICE COLD DRINK,
STARED AT THE DIRTY DISHES,
PILED HIGH IN THE SINK.

HE PASSED THE MIRROR IN THE HALLWAY,
HE GLANCED AS HE WALKED BY,
HE DIDN'T PAUSE TOO LONG
OR HE WOULD SEE A GROWN MAN CRY.

THE SOAP FROM THE SHOWER BURNED
AND STUNG HIS EYES
MEMORIES FLASHED,
HOW HE WOULD LAUGH
TO SEE A GROWN MAN CRY.

HE CHECKED ALL THE MESSAGES,
NO CALLS CAME IN TODAY,
HE STOOD ALONE CRYING
BE CAREFUL WHAT YOU SAY.

THE FAMILY HE ONCE CAME HOME TO, WAS GONE
THEY WALKED AWAY,
THE FIGHTING, LIES AND CHEATING
THEY COULDN'T TAKE ANOTHER DAY.

MEAN WORDS WERE SHOUTED,
HE WISHED HE HAD NEVER SAID,
HE TOSSED THE COLD DAMP TOWEL,
ON THE RUMPLED UNMADE BED.

WHAT DID THE WORLD HAVE TO OFFER?
WHAT WAS HE LOOKING FOR?
HE PONDERED ALL THOSE THOUGHTS,
AS HE PACED AND WALKED THE FLOOR.

HE FELL ON HIS KNEES,
HIS FACE TOWARD THE SKY,
HE DIDN'T CARE WHAT PEOPLE THOUGHT,
IF THEY WOULD SEE A GROWN MAN CRY.

"GIVE ME ONE MORE CHANCE,"
 HE PRAYED TO GOD ABOVE.
"TEACH ME TO BE A MAN,
 TEACH ME TO LOVE."
"TEACH ME NOT TO DESIRE
 THE GRASS ON THE OTHER SIDE."
"TEACH ME TO OBEY YOUR WORD,
 IT WOULD MAKE ME VERY WISE."

"I WOULD LOVE AND CHERISH MY FAMILY,
MY WIFE BY MY SIDE."
A ONCE PROUD MAN,
HUMBLED HIMSELF AND CRIED.

AS HE LAY PROSTRATE ON THE FLOOR,
THE TIME HAD SLIPPED AWAY.
THE NIGHT HAD PASSED ON BY
INTO A BRAND NEW DAY.
IN THE QUIET OF THE MORNING
HE WHISPERED A FEW MORE WORDS,
"THANK YOU LORD,
YOU CHANGED MY HEART,
MY PRAYERS HAVE BEEN HEARD."

HE GOT UP FROM THE FLOOR,
SAT ON THE UNMADE BED,
HE PLACED A CALL TO HIS WIFE,
THIS IS WHAT HE SAID:
"I'M SORRY HOW I'VE TREATED YOU,
I'M SORRY FOR THE THINGS I'VE DONE."
"GOD BLESSED ME WITH A GOOD WIFE,
A DAUGHTER AND A SON."

SHE TOLD HIM SHE HAD PRAYED
THAT HE WOULD MAKE THE CALL,
PRIDE BEFORE DESTRUCTION,
A HAUGHTY SPIRIT BEFORE A FALL.
THE GRASS ON THE OTHER SIDE

MAY LOOK GREENER FROM WHERE
YOU STAND,
BUT JUMPING OVER THE FENCE,
DOESN'T PROVE THAT YOU'RE A MAN.
LOOK AROUND YOUR OWN YARD,
GOD GAVE YOU GREEN GRASS TOO.
TAKE CARE OF IT, NURTURE IT, CUT IT
DON'T LET THE WEEDS GROW HIGH.
A GROWN MAN'S NOT TO BIG
TO STAND ALONE AND CRY.

A LOVING WIFE

THE LORD TOOK A RIB FROM ADAM'S SIDE,
IN HIS AWESOME POWER,
CREATED A BEAUTIFUL BRIDE.
A GLOW IN HER EYES,
LOVE IN HER HEART
WHAT GOD JOINED TOGETHER,
NO MAN COULD TEAR APART.

SHE TRUSTS THE LORD,
IN ALL HER WAYS,
SHE READS HIS WORDS,
SHE ALWAYS PRAYS!
SECURE IN HERSELF,
NOT CONCEITED OR PROUD,
TRULY COMMITTED TO KEEP HER VOWS.

SHE BORE HER CHILDEN,
ANY MOTHER CAN TELL
A JOB THAT'S NOT EASY,
BUT SHE RAISED THEM WELL.
SHE SACFRICED MUCH,
SHE FREELY GAVE.
TRUSTING GOD'S PROMISE,
HER WHOLE HOUSE WOULD BE SAVED.

SHE ACCEPTED THE FAMILY
GOD BLESSED HER WITH,
WHEN THINGS GOT HARD,
SHE WOULD NOT QUIT.
SHE COOKED, SHE CLEANED
SHE DID HER BEST,
HER BURDENS WERE HEAVY
BUT SHE STOOD THE TEST.

SHE PICKED HER BATTLES,
SHE KNEW WHEN TO BE QUIET
AND WHEN TO SPEAK,
CHRIST GAVE HER THE STRENGTH
WHEN HE KNEW SHE WAS WEAK.

A LOVING WIFE...
SHE FIXED THE DISHES HE LIKE TO EAT
RAN THE HOT WATER TO SOAK HIS FEET.
I COULD GO ON AND ON ALL NIGHT,
DON'T FORGET I HAVE THE MIKE.

INSPITE OF ALL SHE HAD TO DO, SHE WORSHIPED
WITH THE SAINTS
ON WEDNESDAYS AND SUNDAYS TOO.

WE SOLUTE YOU MOTHER VALERIE,
WE LOVE YOUR LAUGHER AND BROAD SMILES
ONLY GOD KNEW THE EXTENT OF ALL YOUR TRIALS.

THROUGH LONG HARD DAYS AND LONELY NIGHTS, AT
TIMES YOU FELT
NO HELP WAS IN SIGHT.

WIPE YOUR EYES,
DON'T YOU CRY
SOMEDAY BOBBY WILL BE WAITING IN THE SWEET
BYE AND BYE.
HE WILL PARK THAT BIG BUS AT HEAVEN'S DOOR
AND RIDE YOU AROUND ON A GLORIOUS TOUR.

YOU KEPT THE FAITH,
YOU STUCK BY HIS SIDE.
NO MORE SADNESS,
NO TEARS IN YOUR EYES,
JUST SIT BACK RELAX
AND ENJOY THE RIDE.

A WIFE

A WIFE, A JEWEL AND A FRIEND
(A SOFT HEART)-A WIFE,
(PRECIOUS)-A JEWEL,
(FAITHFUL)-A FRIEND.

THE LORD GOD SAID, "IT'S NOT GOOD THAT
MAN SHOULD BE ALONE."
HE BONDED ADA AND EDCUR WITH LOVE AS
SOLID AS STONE.
EDCUR KNEW IN HIS HEART HE HAD FOUND A REAL
GOOD THING,
TOOK HER HAND IN MARRIAGE,
ON HER FINGER, HE PUT A RING.

GOD SAW THE FUTURE, THE BEGINNING
AND THE END,
HE SAW ADA AS A WIFE, A JEWEL AND A
FAITHFUL FRIEND.
GOD DELIGHTS IN MARRIAGE BETWEEN A WOMAN
AND A MAN.
WHEN THE ENEMY ATTACKED,
HE KNEW ADA WOULD TAKE
A STAND.

SHE PUT HER TRUST IN HIM
IN EVERYTHING SHE DID,

HER FAITH IN THE LORD IS OPEN AND NEVER HID.
HE WAS HER STRENGTH, ON HIM SHE COULD DEPEND,
HE SAW ADA AS A WIFE, A JEWEL AND A
FAITHFUL FRIEND.

AT TIMES TRIALS AND TRIBULATIONS GOT
IN HER WAY,
THE LOVE AND PEACE OF GOD WAS WITH HER
EVERY DAY.
SHE STAYED FAITHFUL UNTIL THE VERY END
GOD SAW HER AS A WIFE, A JEWEL AND A FRIEND.

THROUGH HEALTH, WEALTH AND HARDTIMES
SOMETIMES CONFLICT NEVER ENDS,
ADA WAS A WIFE, A JEWEL AND A FRIEND.

GOD BLESS YOU GROOM AND BRIDE

A SMILE ON YOUR FACE THAT YOU SURELY
CAN'T HIDE.
LOVE IN YOUR HEARTS,
A BRAND NEW START, WHAT GOD HAS JOINED
TOGETHER LET NOT MAN TEAR APART.

GOD LOVES YOU BOTH, HE MAKES ALL THINGS
BRAND NEW, IT SURELY WAS HIS PLAN TO MAKE
YOUR DREAMS TO COME TRUE.
YOUR SPIRITS ARE SO HUMBLE;
YOU ARE ALWAYS SINCERE,
THE SMALLEST WHISPER OF YOUR PRAYERS,
HE SURELY DID HEAR.

AS YOU MOVE ON THE ROAD OF LIFE,
BY EACH OTHERS SIDE
LIKE TEENS GOING TO PROM, WITH TWINKLES IN
YOUR EYES.
AND OH MY- WAIT TILL HE TASTE THAT SWEET
POTATO PIE!

DELICIOUS MEALS TOGETHER
YOU WILL BOTH ENJOY,
JUST LIKE CHILDREN WITH A BRAND NEW TOY!!
HAPPINESS, JOY, AND PEACE YOU DESERVE IT ALL,

THE LORD WON'T FORSAKE YOU AND WON'T
LET YOU FALL.
IN THE MIDST OF YOUR STORMS HOLD ON
TO HIS HAND,
PUT ON ALL OF GOD'S ARMOR SO THAT YOU WILL BE
ABLE TO STAND.

THERE WILL BE GOOD TIMES, BAD TIMES,
SICKNESS AND HEALTH,
YOU MAY BE POOR OR HAVE PLENTY OF WEALTH.
BUT WHEN IT'S ALL SAID AND DONE,
THE WORD SAYS TWO WILL BECOME ONE.

NO MATTER THE SITUATION,
OR WHAT YOU MAY FACE,
REMEMBER GOD HAS THE ANSWER; HE SET THE
STARS IN PLACE.

AS I CLOSE THIS LITTLE POEM DEDICATED TO YOU.
LIFE START A NEW, REMEMBER YOU GO HOME WITH
HIM OR HE GOES HOME WITH YOU. :=)

IT WASN'T MEANT TO BE LIKE THIS

I LISTEN AS THE DOOR CLOSED,
I CRINGED BENEATH THE SHEETS.
I HEARD HIS HEAVY FOOTSTEPS,
I PRETENDED TO BE ASLEEP.

THE BEDROOM DOOR SWUNG OPEN,
GET UP HE SHOUTED AND SCREAMED.
I HUNG MY HEAD IN DISPAIR,
NO PRIDE, NO SELF-ESTEEM.

THE FEAR GRIPPED MY HEART,
AS HE SNATCHED ME FROM THE BED.
THE SMELL OF ALCOHOL,
THE PAINFUL WORDS HE SAID.

IT WAS NEVER MEANT TO BE LIKE THIS,
I DID NOT UNDERSTAND,
HE WAS SUPPOSED TO LOVE AND PROTECT ME,
BE A KIND AND GENTLEMAN.

THE BLOW SENT ME REELING,
BLOOD AND TEARS STUNG MY EYES.
WOULD THIS ONE TAKE ME OUT,
WOULD THIS BE MY DEMISE?

HE DRAGGED ME TO THE KITCHEN,
FLUNG ME TO THE FLOOR.
THE KICKS, SLAPS AND PUNCHES,
NEED I TELL YOU MORE?

THE SCENE WAS REPEATED MORE OFTEN
THAN I CAN TELL.
MY PHONY SMILE TO FRIENDS,
PRETENDING WE'RE DOING WELL.

IT WAS NEVER MEANT TO BE LIKE THIS,
I DID NOT UNDERSTAND.
HE WAS SUPPOSED TO LOVE AND PROTECT ME,
BE A KIND AND GENTLEMAN.

AS FATE WOULD HAVE IT,
AND I MUST TELL IT ALL,
A BURST OF SUDDEN ANGER,
AS MY HEAD HIT THE WALL.

THE KNIFE LAY NEAR MY HAND,
I PLUNGED IT IN HIS CHEST
MY MIND A TOTAL BLURR,
AS THEY PLACED ME
UNDER ARREST.

NO, IT WASN'T SUPPOSE TO BE LIKE THIS,
I MAY NEVER UNDERSTAND,
WHAT HAPPENED TO THE MAN I MET
WITH TENDER LOVING HANDS?

I PONDER ALL THOSE QUESTIONS
AS I SIT IN THIS CELL ALONE,
THE DREAMS OF A HAPPY FAMILY,
LOST
ALL HOPE IS GONE.

LISTEN TO WISE COUNCIL,
A LIFE AND SOUL MIGHT BE SAVED
THE ANSWERS I WAS LOOKING FOR
HE TOOK THEM TO HIS GRAVE.

DON'T PASS THE OPPORTUNITY
TO GET THE HELP YOU NEED,
DON'T WAIT FOR A TOTAL TRAGEDY
TO BRING YOU TO YOUR KNEES.

Author:
Gladys Kneeland
© Oct. 29, 2005

LET GOD MAKE THE CHOICE

WE WERE YOUNG AND IN LOVE, HOW QUICKLY
THINGS DID CHANGE,
NOTHING IS CERTAIN, NOTHING REMAINS THE SAME.
I'M TIRED AND FED UP IS ALL I HAVE TO SAY,
I WANT THIS MAN OUT OF MY LIFE, AND I WANT HIM
GONE TODAY!

YEARS OF UNHAPPINESS HAS TURNED MY
HEART TO STONE,
I KNOW I'LL BE HAPPY IF LEAVES AND NEVER
COMES HOME.

I CAN NO LONGER STAND THE PAIN, AND I DON'T
WANT TO FORGIVE AGAIN,
BEING YOKED WITH A MAN THAT LIVES A LIFE OF SIN.

MY FRIENDS TELL ME TO DIVORCE HIM, TAKE A
FIRM STAND
BE JUST LIKE US, WE DON'T NEED A MAN.

WE ARGUE DAY AND NIGHT PASSING
INSULTING WORDS,
EMBRASSED BY THE THINGS MY CHILDREN AND
FAMILY HEARD.

I WANT TO BE HAPPY; I JUST WANT TO BE FREE,
LORD HEAR MY PRAYER, PLEASE ANSWER ME.

HE QUIETLY SPOKE TO MY SPIRIT.
NOW HEAR WHAT I HAVE TO SAY,
"I'LL TAKE CARE OF THE PROBLEM
IF YOU GET OUT OF THE WAY."

"HAVE YOU FORGOTTEN MY PROMISES?" "MY WORDS
ARE EVER TRUE
THE THINGS YOU CARE ABOUT, I'M WORKING THEM
OUT FOR YOU."

"YOU'VE CRIED AND ASK ME, WHY ARE YOU
TAKING SO LONG?"
"YOU PUT TRUST IN YOUR FRIENDS THAT ONLY LED
YOU WRONG."

"BE STILL AND KNOW ME, I'M NOT A MAN THAT I
SHOULD LIE,
MY WORD SAYS NOT TO WORRY, AND I WILL
TELL YOU WHY."

"PROVERBS 31 IS ALL YOU NEED TO BE, PRAY FOR
YOUR HUSBAND AND HAND HIM OVER TO ME."
"THE YEARS OF LONELINESS AND REGRET YOU
WON'T HAVE TO ENDURE,
TRUST ME AND KNOW THE WORDS OF THE LORD
ARE PURE."

EVERY WISE WOMAN BUILDETH HER HOUSE; BUT
THE FOOLISH PLUCKETH IT DOWN WITH HER HANDS,
THE WICKED ARE OVERTHROWN,
BUT THE HOUSE OF THE RIGHTEOUS SHALL STAND.

"I KNEW THIS DAY WOULD COME,
 I CALLED YOU FROM YOUR MOTHER'S WOMB."
"SURRENDER COMPLETELY TO ME AND YOU WILL
 GET YOU ANSWER SOON."
"AS THE YEARS PASS YOU'LL BE THANKFUL YOU LET
 ME MAKE THE CHOICE,
 I GAVE YOU A BRAND NEW HUSBAND WITHOUT
 A DIVORCE!"

OUR HOUSE - "THE GREENS"

OH THE HAPPY MEMORIES; BUT THERE WERE
SAD ONES TOO.
A FEW OF THE HAPPY MEMORIES I'D LIKE TO
SHARE WITH YOU.

FOUR CHILDREN, MOM AND DAD
IN A LITTLE HOUSE WELL KEPT,
I TRY, BUT CAN'T REMEMBER WHERE IN THE WORLD
WE ALL SLEPT?

SUMMERTIME WAS SO MUCH FUN,
WE HAD MORE LOVE THAN MONEY.
ENTERTAINMENT; IT CAME EASY, FROM
BROTHER SONNY.
WE PLAYED SO HARD, WE LAUGHED, WE BICKERED,
BUT DIDN'T FIGHT,
DAD WOULD YELL EACH NAME UNTIL HE
GOT IT RIGHT.

ON FRIDAYS WHEN DAD GOT PAID, WE RAN TO MEET
HIM AT THE DOOR,
HOPING WE HAD TREATS THAT HE HAD PURCHASED
AT THE STORE.
WE KNEW THERE WAS A SURPRISE TO
SATISFY OUR WISH,

BUT WHEN WE OPEN UP THE BAG, IT CONTAINED
SMOKED FISH. :=(

SATURDAY MORNING MORE FUN, ME AND RALPH,
THE REAL FISHERMEN ON THE PIER,
NO DAD DIDN'T FISH; BUT HE WAS ALWAYS VERY NEAR.

SATURDAY MOVIES
50 CENT TO GET IN 30 CENT FOR POPCORN, WHAT A
TREAT FOR US!
WE DIDN'T COMPLAIN OR EVEN RAISE A FUSS.
I HAD TO TAG ALONG WITH JOYCE; ORDERS
FROM OUR DAD;
THE LOOK ON JOYCE'S FACE, I KNEW IT
MADE HER SAD,
BUT I SKIPPED ALONG SINGING
CHEERFULY AND GLAD.
SUNDAYS
WE PILED IN AN OLD STUDEBAKER SEDAN
OFF TO VISIT
COUSIN STEVE, UNCLE TOM;
A GATHERING OF THE CLAN,
A TREAT ON THE WAY HOME,
AT DAIRY QUEEN'S ICE CREAM STAND.

CHRISTMAS – WAS SPECIAL,
ONE GIFT EACH DAD MADE SURE OF THAT.
A BIG COCONUT CAKE LEFT ON THE TABLE FOR
SANTA ON CHRISTMAS EVE

A SLICE MISSING THE NEXT MORNING, WHAT OTHER
TRICKS WAS UP THEIR SLEEVE??

THE LITTLE HOUSE ON ELIZABETH STILL
REMAINS TODAY,
TIMES HAVE PASSED WE'RE ALL GROWN AND GONE
OUR SEPARATE WAY.
THE MEMORIES IN THAT LITTLE HOUSE EACH ONE
OF US HAS KEPT.
I TRY, BUT CAN'T REMEMBER WHERE IN THE WORLD
WE ALL SLEPT??????

GLADYS KNEELAND

THE MARRIAGE JOURNEY

GOD BLESS YOU BEAUTIFUL COUPLE AS YOU STAND
HAND IN HAND. THE PERFECT UNION GOD DESIGNED;
A LADY AND A MAN.
AS YOU PREPARE YOUR JOURNEY TOGETHER, TWO
HAVE BECOME ONE.
THE ROAD PAVED WITH UNKNOWNS, HAS ONLY
JUST BEGUN.
THERE WILL BE LAUGHTER, GOOD TIMES, BAD
TIMES SUNSHINE AND RAIN.

TAKE THE TRIP TOGETHER, NOT WITH FAMILY
OR FRIENDS AVOIDING THE EXTRA PAIN. THE
FEWER DRIVERS AT THE WHEEL, THE BETTER OFF
YOU'LL BE.
THERE WILL BE PATHS OF DISSAPOINTMENTS AND
ACCOMPLISHMENTS TOO. BUMPY AND SMOOTH
TRAILS WILL BE WAITING FOR YOU.

MISUNDERSTANDINGS AROUND THE CORNER
HOLDING A SIGN THAT SAYS YIELD,
COMMUNICATION COMING THROUGH, NO MATTER
HOW YOU FEEL.

BEWARE OF THE SHARP CURVES, DANGER AHEAD;
DON'T DETOUR BECAUSE OF GOSSIP OR SOMETHING

SOMEONE SAID. SLIPPERY WHEN WET CAN CAUSE
YOU TO CRASH.
YOU CAN'T DRIVE LOOKING BACK, SO LET GO
OF THE PAST.

CAUTION THERE'S A FLASHING YELLOW LIGHT JUST
OVER THE HILL TAKE THE ROAD OF UNDERSTAND
CONCERNING BUSINESS AND BILLS.

AS YOU MANEUVER OVER THE MILES THERE WILL BE
ROAD BLOCKS POTHOLES AND NEW CONSTRUCTION
TOO, PEOPLE WILL LOOK DIFFERENT FROM THE DAY
THEY SAID I DO.
DON'T LET OUTSIDE INFLUENCES CAUSE YOU
TO SWITCH.
THE BLIND CAN'T LEAD THE BLIND OR THEY WILL
BOTH FALL IN A DITCH.

GOD IS THE CO-PILOT HE HAS PLOTTED YOUR
PATH WHEN HE IS IN CONTROL YOUR MARRIAGE
WILL LAST.
HE KNOWS YOUR DESIRES, AND HE KNOWS
YOUR HEART.
WHAT GOD HAS PUT TOGETHER, LET NO MAN
TEAR APART.

MAMA

AS A CHILD, I FAILED TO SEE HOW MUCH MY MAMA
CARED FOR ME.
SHE WOULD HOLD ME TENDERLY IN HER ARMS,
SHIELDING ME FROM ALL DANGER AND HARM.
AS A CHILD, I DID NOT KNOW THAT EXTRA MILE
MAMA WOULD GO.
SHE WOULD FIX THAT SPECIAL HOME COOKED DISH;
IT SATISFIED MY EVERY WISH.

SHE DRESSED ME IN NICE WARM CLOTHES, GAVE ME
CASTOR OIL FOR MY RUNNY NOSE.
AS A CHILD MAMA TOOK SUCH SPECIAL CARE; SHE
WASHED, SHE COMBED AND SHE PLATTED MY HAIR.
EACH DAY SHE SENT ME OFF TO SCHOOL,
TOLD ME TO FOLLOW THE GOLDEN RULE.

SHE COOKED, SHE CLEANED, SHE BABY SAT TOO;
SEEMED LIKE MAMA'S WORK WAS NEVER THROUGH.
AS A CHILD I COULD NOT FIGURE OUT HOW MAMA
ALWAYS KNEW ALL THOSE TRICKS I TRIED TO DO.

THOSE TRICKS I TRIED TO DO.
SHE KNEW ALL I DID AND ALL I SAID. DID MAMA
HAVE EYES IN THE BACK OF HER HEAD?
SHE KNEW HOW TO CALM ME WHEN I'D POUT,
IN A WAY I WOULDN'T FORGET,

BECAUSE I NEEDED A PILLOW WHEN I'D SIT.

AS A CHILD I WOULD
SOMETIMES SAY,
"WHY DOES IT HAVE TO BE THIS WAY?"
WHEN MAMA SAID NO, I WANTED IT YES, NEVER
REALIZING THAT MAMA KNEW BEST.

AS A CHILD, I ALWAYS HEARD MAMA'S ADVICE; MORE
THAN ONCE, MORE THAN TWICE.
"WHAT GOES AROUND COMES AROUND, MAMA
WOULD SAY, SO TREAT SOMEONE NICE TODAY."
"IF YOU DIG ONE DITCH, YOU MIGHT AS WELL DIG
TWO, ONE FOR THEM AND ONE FOR YOU."

"BOUGHT SENSE IS THE BEST SENSE, JUST YOU
WAIT AND SEE."
NONE OF MAMA'S WORDS WERE CLEAR TO ME.

AS A CHILD I DID NOT REALIZE THE TEARS THAT
FELL FROM MAMA'S EYES; WERE SOMETIMES OF
JOY, SOMETIMES OF PAIN.
SHE NEVER TOOK THE TIME TO EXPLAIN.
SHE WOULD JUST WIPE HER HANDS ON HER APRON
AND SAY, "ALL YOU KIDS GO OUT AND PLAY."

NOW I LOOK BACK I UNDERSTAND, MAMA WAS LED
BY GOD'S OWN HAND.

THROUGH ALL THE TEARS, THE JOY, THE PAIN, I
KNOW MAMA'S PRAYERS WERE NOT IN VAIN.

I WOULD HEAR MAMA SAY, "I WON'T ALWAYS BE
HERE, SO LISTEN VERY CAREFULLY DEAR." "THE
ADVICE I SO LOVINGLY GAVE, WILL SOONER OR
LATER SPEAK UP FROM MY GRAVE."
"WHEN YOU WANT TO TALK TO MAMA AND
MAMA CAN'T HEAR, CALL ON THE LORD, HE'S
ALWAYS NEAR."

NO MATTER WHAT YOU GO THROUGH OR HARD IT
WILL BE. REMEMBER, GOD'S WORD IS THE ANSWER,
HE HOLDS THE KEY.
THANK THE LORD; HE GAVE MAMA TO ME!!

FRIENDSHIP

MY FRIEND HERMAN

TWO GOOD FRIENDS—-

ON SEPARATE PATHS OF LIFE,
SEPARATE WORLDS APART,
WAS IT FATE THAT CAUSED OUR PATHS TO CROSS,
OR WAS IT A TUGGING OF OUR HEARTS?

HOW LIFE'S PATHS TWIST AND TURN,
WE DO NOT KNOW,
AND WILL NEVER UNDERSTAND.
GOD HOLDS THE FUTURE,
IT'S ALL IN HIS HANDS.

IF THE CHOICE WERE MINE,
I WOULD TRAVEL LIFE'S PATH WITH YOU.
I WOULD HELP YOU UP WHEN YOU FALL,
CAUSE THAT'S WHAT REAL FRIENDS DO.

THERE WILL BE CLOUDS MIXED WITH SUNSHINE,
UNTIL THE PATHS OF LIFE ENDS.
MY PRAYERS IS THAT
WE WILL ALWAYS REMAIN

TWO GOOD FRIENDS—

LOVE,
GLADYS

A MAN CALLED PETER

HOW I CAME TO KNOW HIM IS A MYSTERY TO ME
GOD WORKED OUT THE DETAILS
FROM FAR ACROSS THE SEA.

THE TALES OF HIS HUMBLE BEGINNINGS
AT TIMES HIS PATIENCE TRIED
THE HARDSHIPS HE ENDURED
BROUGHT TEARS TO MY EYES.

THE DISAPPOINTMENTS HE EXPIERENCED
DIDN'T HINDER HIM AT ALL
HE STAYED STRONG,
HE KEPT THE FAITH,
NOTHING CAUSED HIM TO FALL.

HE STUDIED LONG HARD HOURS
SPENT LONELY DAYS AND NIGHTS
DETERMINED TO MAKE IT
HE KEPT HIS GOAL IN SIGHT.

HOUR AFTER HOUR
HE SPENT IN THE
SCHOOL LAB
WITH PATIENCE AND ENDURANCE
NO ONE ELSE COULD HAVE.

HE SHARED HIS HOPES AND DREAMS
STAYED FOCUSED UNTIL THE END
LISTEN TO WORDS OF WISDOM FROM WISE AND
GODLY MEN.

BLESSED WITH MANY TALENTS
HE WEARS MANY HATS
AN ACCOMPLISHED MINISTER OF MUSIC
I KNOW GOD HAS HIS BACK.

A MAN CALLED PETER
WITH A MILLION DOLLAR SMILE
SERIOUS ABOUT HIS WORK
HE WILL GO THE EXTRA MILE.

HE LEAVES A LASTING IMPRESSION
WITH EVERYONE HE MEETS
IF HIS ENEMY IS HUNGRY, HE WOULD GIVE HIM
BREAD TO EAT.

I AM HONORED TO KNOW HIM
PROUD TO BE HIS FRIEND
HIS INTEGRITY IMPECCABLE
ON THAT YOU CAN DEPEND.

A MAN CALLED PETER
VERY BRILLIANT AND SMART
SKILLED IN HIS PROFESSION
YOU CAN TRUST HIM WITH YOUR HEART.

WHEN HE MEETS THAT SPECIAL PERSONAND GIVES
HER A RING
WHAT JOY,
IT WILL MAKE HIS
HEART SING.

A MAN CALLED PETER
NO MATTER WHERE HE GOES
I KNOW HE WILL SUCCEED
HE CAN STAND AND FACE
THE WORLD
IF HE STAYS ON HIS KNEES.

FRIENDS...

SATURDAY NIGHT WAS OVER,
IT HAD ALL COME TO AN END.
SHE PROMISED HER CHILDREN,
I'LL LEAVE THIS WORLD OF SIN.

SHE DIDN'T FEEL VERY GOOD
THAT MORNING,
AS SHE PACED AND WALKED THE FLOOR,
AWAKEN FROM HER DAY DREAM
BY A KNOCK AT THE DOOR.

"WON'T YOU JOIN ME AT CHURCH THIS EVENING
THERE'S SOMETHING YOU MUST SEE,
A MAN WHO WORKS FOR JESUS,
PRAYING TO SET THE CAPTIVE FREE."

"YES," SHE REPLIED
HOPING THE VISITOR WOULD NOT STAY,
SHE HAD TO GET BACK TO HER PROBLEMS
AND THE CARES OF THE DAY.

THAT EVENING SHE WENT TO SERVICE,
SHE HAD NOTHING ELSE GO DO,
BESIDES WATCHING ALL THOSE SAINTS,
MIGHT GIVE HER A LAUGH OR TWO.

SOMEONE PULLED HER IN THE PRAYER LINE,
SURROUNDED HER ON EACH SIDE
"WE'LL LOVE YOU, WE'LL SHEILD YOU,
WE'LL BE YOUR SPIRITUAL GUIDE."

I CAN TELL THEM MY PROBLEMS,
I KNOW THEY'LL LEND A HAND
I CAN TELL THEM MY SECRETS
I KNOW THEY'LL UNDERSTAND.

THE PHONE CALLS KEPT HER ENCOURAGED.
"STAY PRAYFULL," WERE WORDS SHE WOULD HEAR;
I'VE TRADED MY OLD LIFE FOR FRIENDS THAT
ARE SO DEAR!

THE WEEKS PASSED QUICKLY
THE PHONE.....
IT DIDN'T RING SO MUCH,
EACH DAY SHE WOULD CALL HER FRIENDS WITH
WHOM SHE COULD NOT GET IN TOUCH.

AT CHURCH THE SMILES GREW FEWER,
GROUPS STOOD HUDDLED TO THE SIDE,
I'M IN THIS WALK ALONE
AS TEARS FILLED HER EYES.

I'LL GO BACK TO THE DARKNESS
A WORLD WHERE SHE HAD BEEN,
OUT THERE SHE KNEW FOR SURE

THAT NO ONE IS YOUR FRIEND.

IF I LED SOMEONE TO JESUS,
GOD'S ONLY SON,
I WOULD TELL THEM DON'T LOOK TO FRIENDS,
BECAUSE TOMORROW THEY'LL BE GONE.

SHE SAT ON HER BED PRAYING,
"LORD I HURT SO BAD,
WHY DID THEY BETRAY ME?"
"THEY WERE ALL THE FRIENDS I HAD."
GOD ANSWER, IT CAME QUICKLY
"YOU'RE MINE AND IN MY HAND
"YOUR FAITH LIES IN ME,
SURELY NOT IN MAN."

"I WILL FILL YOU WITH MY SPIRIT,
GIVE YOU POWER FROM ABOVE,
SHOWER YOU WITH BLESSINGS,
FILL YOUR HEART WITH LOVE."
"I WILL GIVE YOU VICTORY,
WHICH NO MAN HOLDS THE KEY,
BUT THAT WILL ONLY COME
MY CHILD WHEN YOU TOTALLY DEPEND ON ME!!"

POWER OF THE TONGUE

WE COULD BORE EACH OTHER WITH OUR WOES,
WONDERING, WHERE COULD HAPPINESS BE.
WE COULD HELP EACH OTHER CRY,
SHARE SOME SYMPATHY.

WE COULD TALK ABOUT OUR PROBLEMS,
THE STORIES WOULD GO ON AND ON
OUR BILLS ARE DUE,
OUR RELATIONSHIPS,
OUR DAUGHTERS
AND OUR SONS.

WE COULD TALK ABOUT OUR ISSUES,
THEY PLAGUE US DAY AND NIGHT.
SEEMS THERE'S NO HOPE
AND HOW WE FRET
WITH JUST NO END IN SIGHT.

WE COULD TALK ABOUT HOW WE'VE BEEN
MIS-TREATED,
AND LIFE IS SO UNFAIR,
HOW WE CRY, AND WE CAN'T SLEEP
OUR BURDENS TO HARD TO BEAR.

WE COULD TELL THE LATEST GOSSIP, WHAT GOOD
WOULD THAT DO?
SPREADING THINGS WE'VE HEARD

THAT PROBABLY AREN'T EVEN TRUE.

WE COULD SIT ALL NICE AND QUIET,
LISTENING TO WHAT OTHERS SAY.
AFRAID SOMEONE WILL ASK,
"WHAT PROBLEMS CAME YOUR WAY?"

WE ALL KNOW ABOUT PAIN AND SORROW,
AND YES THE HURT IS REAL.
NO ONE KNOWS WHERE WE'VE BEEN
OR JUST HOW BAD WE FEEL.

"JUST GET OVER IT."
A PHRASE WE OFTEN HEAR
COMING FROM FAMILY AND
FRIENDS,
SHOUTED IN OUR EAR.
WE GO ON SINGING THE BLUES,
WHO KNOWS OUR TRIALS,
OR WHOSE WALKED IN OUR SHOES?

GOD LEFT US HERE FOR A PURPOSE.
NO MATTER WHAT HAS HAPPENED,
OR HOW FIERCE THE FIGHT,
HOW BAD WE FEEL WHEN THINGS AREN'T
GOING RIGHT.

THE ENEMY MAY HAVE STOLE OUR JOY,
HE'S ON HIS JOB,
TO STEAL, KILL AND DESTROY.

NO MATTER
HOW LOW THE VALLEY SEEMS,
IT MAY HAVE RAINED ON OUR PARADE,
IT RAINED ON OUR PARADE WE'VE ALL HAD
AND BROKEN ALL OUR DREAMS.

GOD IS IN CONTROL OF OUR LIVES
THE THINGS WE DO NOT UNDERSTAND,
JUST DON'T GIVE UP,
KEEP TRUSTING.
IT'S ALL IN HIS HANDS.

SO WHILE WE'RE HERE
LET'S FOCUS ON HIS GOODNESS
TAKE LIFE A DAY AT A TIME,
PRESS ON TOWARD THE MARK
LEAVE OUR SITUATIONS BEHIND.
LET'S GIVE GOD THE PRAISE
THERE'S NEW SONGS TO BE SUNG.
REMEMBER
DEATH AND LIFE ARE IN THE
POWER OF THE TONGUE!!!

Psalm 145:14
The Lord upholds all who fall, and raises up all who are
bowed down.

REFLECTIONS

A MAN SAT BY THE SEA SHORE,
REFLECTING ON HIS LIFE.
THE GOOD TIMES, THE BAD TIMES,
HIS CHILDREN AND HIS WIFE.

HE THOUGHT ABOUT HIS CHILDHOOD,
HOW HAPPY HE HAD BEEN.
HE THOUGHT ABOUT SOME PAINFUL TIMES
HE WOULDN'T WANT TO RELIVE AGAIN.

HE THOUGHT ABOUT HIS TEENAGE YEARS
FULL OF LAUGHTER AND FUN.
HE THOUGHT ABOUT THE
MISCHEVIOUS AND CRUEL THINGS HE HAD DONE.

HE THOUGHT ABOUT THE PEOPLE HE HAD KNOWN,
THOSE WHO HAD COME
AND THOSE WHO HAD GONE.

HE PONDERED ON HIS MISTAKES,
AND THE FAILURES HE WENT THROUGH,
HE THOUGHT ABOUT HIS SUCCESSES
AND HIS GOOD DECISIONS TOO.

HE THOUGHT ABOUT ALL THE YEARS,
HOW QUICKLY THEY HAD PASSED,

QUALITY TIME WITH HIS WIFE
HAD FINALLY COME AT LAST.

A TIME FOR THE TWO OF THEM
TO TAKE A MUCH NEEDED REST,
A HOUSE ONCE BUBBLING WITH NOISE
HAD BECOME AN EMPTY NEST.

HE THOUGHT ABOUT THE DOCTOR'S NEWS,
AND NO,
IT WASN'T GOOD,
A TEAR FELL FROM HIS EYE,
LORD, I WISH I UNDERSTOOD.

FINALLY, HE THOUGHT HARD ABOUT HIS LIFE,
WONDERING WHY HE WAS HERE,
HE BOWED HIS HEAD AND PRAYED,
"LORD MAKE MY PURPOSE CLEAR."

AS HE SAT IN THE STILLNESS,
IT WAS QUIET AND SERENE,
A STILL SMALL VOICE SPOKE FROM THE SEA
AS THOUGH IT WAS A DREAM.

"CAST ALL OF YOUR CARES ON GOD BECAUSE HE
CARES FOR YOU,"
HE CREATED YOU FOR A PURPOSE,
AND THERE IS WORK FOR YOU TO DO."

"VISIT A LONELY SENIOR,
 BRING JOY TO A HURTING SOUL,
 TELL A FUNNY STORY THE WAY IT'S NEVER
 BEEN TOLD."
"STOP BY A SHELTER,
 HELP IN THE FOOD LINE,
 VOLUNTEER IN A HOSPITAL,
 HOLD THE HAND OF SOMEONE BLIND."
"MENTOR A CHILD
 WHOSE FATHER HAS WALKED AWAY,
 TEACH HIM A VALUABLE SKILL,
 HELP HIM NOT TO GO ASTRAY."

THE THINGS YOU CAN DO FOR OTHERS,
THE LIST GOES ON AND ON.
THE REWARDS;
PEACE AND JOY HAVE ONLY JUST BEGUN.

YOU'LL FORGET ABOUT YOUR PROBLEMS,
THEY WILL ALL SEEM TO END,
GOD RESTORED JOB TO HEALTH,
WHEN HE PRAYED FOR HIS FRIENDS.

GOD HAS HEARD YOUR PRAYERS,
HE HAS BOTTLED EVERY TEAR,
HE PROMISED IN HIS WORD,
HE WOULD ALWAYS BE NEAR.

WHEN YOU'RE FEELING
SAD AND THE QUESTION
IS ALWAYS WHY?
HARKEN TO HIS VOICE,
HE'S NOT A MAN THAT HE SHOULD LIE.

HE WALKED AWAY FROM THE QUIET SEA,
WITH NEW HOPE AND A BRAND NEW START,
HE WALKED WITH NEW DIRECTION,
AND ENCOURAGEMENT IN HIS HEART.

HOLD FAST TO GOD'S WORD,
NOT YOUR FORTUNES AND YOUR WEALTH,
YES, GOD WANTS YOU TO PROSPER AND BE IN
GOOD HEALTH.

WRITE DOWN GOD'S HEALING SCRIPTURES AND
QUOTE THEM EVERYDAY,
THERE'S POWER IN THE WORD OF GOD,
YOU WILL HAVE JUST WHAT YOU SAY!

FUNERALS

A JEWEL

GOD CREATED A JEWEL MORE PRECIOUS
THAN DIAMONDS,
SILVER OR GOLD
A JEWEL SO RARE,
NOT TO BE BOUGHT OR SOLD.
"WHAT DID YOU CALL THE JEWEL
THE ANGELS INQUIRED?"
"ANNIE EASLEY OF COURSE,
SHE WILL BE GREATLY ADMIRED."

"I PLACED LOVE IN HER HEART THAT COULD NOT
BE COMPARED
HER BLESSING AND TALENTS SHE WOULD
ALWAYS SHARE."

DID YOU PLACE HER WITH OTHERS?"
THE QUESTIONS NEVER SEEMED TO END.
"I SURROUNDED HER WITH A LARGE FAMILY AND
MANY, MANY FRIENDS."

"OH YOU MUST HAVE LOVED HER!"
"YES SHE WAS SPECIAL YOU SEE;
THE WAY SHE TREATED OTHERS
SHE DID IT UNTO TO ME."
"IF HER ENEMY WAS HUNGRY, SHE GAVE HIM BREAD
TO EAT; IF HE WAS THIRSTY, SHE GAVE HIM A DRINK,

REGARDLESS OF NAYSAYERS OR WHAT THEY
WOULD THINK."

"MY JEWEL WILL LAY THE FOUNDATION
 FOR MANY TO BE BLESSED;
 THE SACFRACIES
 AND TRIALS, I KNEW SHE WOULD PASS THE TEST."
"THE SPARKLE THAT WOULD RADIATE FROM HER
 ALL WILL SEE,
 HER REWARD DIDN'T COME FROM MAN,
 IT CAME FROM ME."

"I SET HER BOUNDS ACCORDING TO MY WORD;
 WHICH IS ALWAYS TRUE,
 I KNEW SHE WOULD SET THE STAGE
 AND BE THE FAMILY'S GLUE."

"MY JEWEL WILL LEAVE AN IMPRESSION
 ON MANY THAT CROSS HER PATH;
 SOWING SEEDS OF KINDNESS;
 CAUSING HER MEMORY TO LAST."

"FRUITS OF THE SPIRIT, PEACE, PATIENCE GOODNESS
 AND GENTLENESS IN EVERY WAY,
 THE MORE SHE GAVE OUT;
 SIMPLY MADE HER DAY."
THE WORDS USED TO DESCRIBE HER ARE ONLY
A FEW, YES
PROVERBS 31 FITS HER TOO!

GOD'S PRECIOUS JEWEL SHOULD BE AN EXAMPLE
IN OUR LIFE; IMITATORS OF HER AS SHE
FOLLOWED CHRIST.
HIS COMMAND TO LOVE
AND TREAT EACH OTHER RIGHT,

THE LORD PLACED HIS PRECIOUS JEWEL ON A SHIP
THAT SAILED OUT OF SIGHT.
PLEASE DON'T FRET
BECAUSE HER JOURNEY DIDN'T END
AS SHE SAILES ON WITH JESUS,
SHE JUST TURNED THE BEND.

THE ANGELS AT THE HELM LEADING THE WAY
NO MORE QUESTIONS;
ALL THEY COULD SAY.
"NOW WE KNOW;
WE UNDERSTAND WHY;
YOUR PRECIOUS JEWEL,
THE APPLE OF YOUR EYE."
LIFT UP YOUR HEADS MY LOVE ONES AND BE
HAPPY FOR ME,
RIDING AROUND HEAVEN,
IT'S WHERE I WANT TO BE;
ANGELS AND I STOPPING AT EVERY FLEA
MARKET WE SEE!!

THE MIRACLE OF LOVE

THE MIRACLE OF LOVE
WE WILL NEVER UNDERSTAND
HOW GOD WRITES THE SCRIPT
FOR A WOMAN AND A MAN.
IN HIS WISDOM, HE SETS THE STAGE.
HE BROUGHT DORIS AND CURLEY TOGETHER
AT A VERY EARLY AGE.

CURLEY FOUND DORIS
AT THE AGE OF 17,
WITH LOVE IN HIS HEART,
HE CHOSE HER TO BE HIS QUEEN.
THE TWO BECAME ONE,
GOD BLESSED THEIR UNION WITH
2 DAUGHTERS AND 3 SONS.

THE MIRACLE OF LOVE
KEPT THEM TOGETHER
NO MATTER WHAT CAME THEIR WAY,
THEY TOOK THEIR PROBLEMS TO THE ALTER
AND THAT'S WHERE THEY WOULD STAY.
GOD WROTE THEIR SCRIPT,
THE CAST WAS COMPLETE,
CURLEY AND DORIS
WERE IN IT FOR KEEPS.

DORIS HAD HER BOAZ
SHE TREATED HIM LIKE A KING,
THE LOVE HE SHOWED HER
SIMPLY MADE HER HEART SING.
SHE WAS CURLEY'S PRINCES BRIDE,
THE THOUGHT OF HER VIRTUE
MADE HIM BUBBLE WITH PRIDE.

CURLEY HAD A QUIET SPIRIT
PLEASE DON'T GET IT WRONG,
WHEN IT CAME TO STRENGTH
HE WASN'T WEAK, BUT STRONG.
THEY LOVED THEIR CHILDREN
AND TAUGHT THEM WHAT WAS RIGHT,
BUT IF ANYONE HARMED THEM
CURLEY WAS IN THE FIGHT.

FOR RICHER, FOR POORER, IN SICKNESS AND
HEALTH. THE LOVE THEY SHARED, MORE PRECIOUS
THAN WEALTH.
A LOVE SO SECURE, THEY HAD EACH OTHER'S BACK,
WITHSTOOD THE ENEMY
IF UNDER ATTACK.
CURLEY SERVED HIS COUNTRY,
HE TRAVELED THE NATIONWIDE
NO MATTER WHERE HE WENT,
HIS WIFE AND CHILDREN BY HIS SIDE.
WHEN DUTY CALLED, CURLEY WAS THERE
EARNED THE BRONZE STAR,

AND MEDALS HE WAS PROUD TO WEAR.

I'VE SAID MUCH ABOUT THEIR LOVE
WHICH NO ONE CAN DENY,
THEY TRAVELED THE GLORY TRAIN TOGETHER
TO THE SWEET BYE AND BYE.
ANGELS GREETED THEM AND WELCOMED THEM
TO BE WITH THE LORD
LAY OUT THE RED CARPET,
A CROWN OF JEWELS THEIR AWARD.

CURLEY AND DORIS WORKED HARD,
THEY DID THEIR BEST.
NOW THEY'RE RELAXING IN THE SUNSHINE
FOR AN ETERNAL REST.

THE MIRACLE OF LOVE
THEY STOOD, AND DID NOT QUIT,
ENTERED THE RACE,
SET THEIR FACE.
THE CURTAIN HAS CLOSED,
THE ARCHANGEL GABRIEL
ANNOUNCED THEIR NAME
AS THEY STROLL THE HEAVENLY WALK OF FAME.

GOD IN HIS WISDOM MADE THE RIGHT CHOICE
PLEASE DON'T BE SAD,
REJOICE, REJOICE!!

BRO JOHN

THE WORD DASH HAS NUMEROUS MEANINGS;
ONE MEANING - TO DASH OFF, TO HURRY AWAY.

THE DASH REFERRED TO IN MOST EULOGIES IS THE
SHORT TIME BETWEEN BIRTH AND DEATH.
IT SOMETIMES SEEMS THAT'S HOW LIFE IS: WE
HURRAY AWAY.
JOB 14:1 READS "MAN THAT IS BORN OF A WOMAN IS
OF FEW DAYS AND FULL OF TROUBLE."

I DID NOT KNOW BRO. JOHN FROM THE BEGINNING
OF HIS DASH;
I'D LIKE TO BRIEFLY DESCRIBE THE PART OF THE
DASH I KNEW.

THE "D" DOING WHAT IS RIGHT, A SMILE AND KIND
WORDS TO SAY,
HE WAS GENEROUS AND HELPING
OTHERS ALONG THE WAY.
WORKING FOR THE UNDERPRIVILIGED -
WHENEVER HE COULD,
I KNOW GOD SMILED DOWN; SAYING "BRO. JOHN
THAT WAS GOOD."
IF THERE WERE A NEED, HE WOULD EXTEND HIS
HAND TO YOU,
YES, THAT'S THE BRO. JOHN I KNEW.

129

THE "A" ASKING GOD TO GUIDE HIM, PRAISING HIM EVERYDAY!!
GOD IS IN CONTROL; THAT'S WHAT HE WOULD SAY.
WITH LOVE, HE PRAYED FOR HIS FAMILY, FRIENDS AND STRANGERS TOO,
ASKING GOD TO BLESS, KEEP AND CARRY THEM SAFELY THROUGH.
THAT'S THE BRO. JOHN I KNEW.

THE "S" SILENT AND SERENE –
NOT JUDGING OR COMPLAINING, HE WAS FORGIVING WITH A HEART PURE AND TRUE,
A QUIET AND GENTLE SPIRIT
YES, THAT'S THE BRO. JOHN I KNEW.

THE "H" HUMILITY, HE WAS HUMBLE,
HE SAID TRUSTING IN GOD TO HELP HIM RUN THE RACE,
HIS LIFE WAS IN GOD'S HANDS, NO MATTER WHAT HE FACED.
HE SAID HIS SEAT WAS RESERVED IN GLORY
AND HE WAS FINE WITH WHATEVER GOD WOULD DO
THAT'S THE BRO. JOHN I KNEW.

THE DASH YOU KNEW MAY NOT BE DESCRIBED
LIKE MINE,
WE ALL WILL HAVE A DASH; IT'S JUST A
MATTER OF TIME.
HOW WILL OUR DASH BE DESCRIBED, WHAT WILL
OTHERS SAY?
WILL THEIR REPORT BE TRUE?
AND DO WE SEE OURSELVES JUST AS OTHERS DO?

LET THE LOVE AND GRACE OF GOD LIVE IN
OUR HEART,
ALL THE OLD HE WILL MAKE NEW.
I PRAY THE DASH I SAW IN BRO. JOHN
SOMEONE WILL SEE IN ME AND YOU.

MATTIE

GOD PLANTED A FLOWER GARDEN;
HE PLACED MATTIE THERE TO GROW.
SHELTERED HER FROM THE ELEMENTS, WIND,
RAIN AND SNOW.
MATTIE BLOSSOMED RIGHT FROM THE START.
HE GAVE HER A SMILE - THAT TRULY CAPTURED
YOUR HEART.

HE NUTURED HER EVERYDAY,
SHE GREW TO LOVE OTHER FLOWERS
IN A VERY SPECIAL WAY.
HE PULLED WEEDS
FROM THE GARDEN,
WHEN SHE HAD NO STRENGTH TO ENDURE;
THE LOVE OF GOD SURROUNDED HER MADE HER
FEEL SECURE.

THE GARDEN CONTAINED
FAMILY THAT SHE THOUGHT
THE WORLD OF
SPECIAL IN HER HEART;
SENT FROM GOD ABOVE.

CHILDREN GREW IN THE GARDEN;
IRVING, NINA AND SHENELL.

A SLEW OF GRANDCHILDREN SHE ADORED
THEM AS WELL.
MATTIE WOULD TACKLE SOME HARD TIMES, BUT
NO MATTER WHAT CAME HER WAY
GOD HAD HER BACK;
HE HAD THE LAST SAY.

OCTOBER 28, 2012
GOD REACHED DOWN FROM HEAVEN; HE PICKED
MATTIE FROM THE FLOWER GARDEN
AND BROUGHT HER BY HIS SIDE.
NO MORE BURDENS,
NO MORE, TOILING
NO MORE TEARS TO BE CRIED.

MATTIE WILL BE MISSED,
BY HER FAMILY
AND HER FRIENDS;
THE MEMORY OF HER LAUGH
WILL NEVER COME TO AN END.

WALKING IN THE GARDEN WITH JESUS,
SHE WOULD PROBABLY SAY;
BELIEVE ON CHRIST THE SAVIOR
AND YOU'LL BE WALKING WITH US ONE DAY.

SORROW

WE'RE SORRY THAT YOU LEFT US,
WE'RE SORRY YOU WENT AWAY.
YOU WERE SO VERY CLOSE
JUST THE OTHER DAY.

WE'RE SORRY WE DIDN'T SAY I LOVE YOU;
MORE OFTEN THAN WE DID,
WE'RE SORRY ALL THOSE FEELINGS
WE SO CLOSELY HID.

WE'RE SORRY WE DIDN'T SPEND MORE TIME TO TALK
AND LOOK YOU IN THE EYE,
WE'RE SORRY LIFE IS SHORT,
IT GOES SO QUICKLY BY.

WE'RE SORRY WE CAN'T HEAR YOU SINGING
AND YOUR LAUGHTER AS YOU USE TO DO;
PLAYING BALL WITH ALL THE CHILDREN,
THEY WILL MISS YOU TOO!

WE'RE SORRY OUR TEARS WON'T BRING YOU BACK,
WE'RE ALL VERY SORRY, WHAT MORE CAN WE SAY,
JUST SAYING SORRY WON'T TAKE THE TEARS AWAY.

WE'RE SORRY LIFE HAS PAIN THAT WE CAN NOT
HARDLY BEAR,
WE'RE SORRY THAT YOU LEFT US,
AND THESE WORDS WE CAN NOT SHARE.

SO WE'RE SORRY WE DIDN'T TELL YOU MORE
THE LOVE WE
HAVE FOR YOU,
WE DIDN'T SHARE HOW MUCH
GOD LOVED YOU TOO!!

BUT IN ALL OUR SORROW, THERE'S GOD
BY OUR SIDE;
HE'LL HEAL ALL OUR PAIN AND WIPE THE TEARS
FROM OUR EYES.

WE SHARE PLEASANT MEMORIES OF YOU;
WITH GOD BY OUR SIDE, WE KNOW WE'LL MAKE
IT THROUGH.

ZENOBIA RANDOLPH

IF I WERE TO WRITE ZENOBIA RANDOLPH'S EULOGY,
IT WOULD GO SOMETHING LIKE THIS:
SHE LEFT PORT IN APRIL 1925;
SAILED ON THROUGH LIFE,
HER JOURNEY UNDERWAY;
MARRIED RAISED A FAMILY,
ATTRACTED FRIENDS AND LOVE ONES EVERYDAY.
THE STORMS OF LIFE CAUSED STRONG GALES
AND FIERCE WINDS,
BUT SHE BOTTENED DOWN THE HATCH
AND SAILED ON AGAIN.

SHE SAILED THROUGH THE LOSS OF LOVED ONES,
WAVES BEAT HARD AGAINST THE BOW.
EMBARKED ON UNKNOWN TERRITORY,
WITH FAITH, SHE MADE IT THROUGH SOMEHOW.

SHE SAILED THROUGH SICKNESS SET
PORT AT UNKNOWN SHORES,
BUT SHE KNEW WHO WAS AT THE HELM,
WHO GAVE HER STRENGTH TO ENDURE.
CAPTAIN JESUS GAVE THE ORDER JANUARY 2010,
LOWER THE ANCHOR, TAKE YOUR REST;
IT'S TIME TO COME ON IN.

DOCK YOUR SHIP AT SHORE,

CAPTAIN JESUS IS SMILING
AS HE WAITS AT HEAVEN'S DOOR.
WELL DONE GOOD AND FAITHFUL SERVANT,
FOREVER WITH ME YOU'LL DWELL,
A CROWN OF GLORY WITH A PURPLE HEART,
YOU REPRESENTED ME WELL!!

MISCELLANEOUS POEMS

A PRECIOUS CHILD

I HIT HER ONE MORE TIME,
"QUIET, I WOULD SCREAM,
YOU'RE GETTING ON MY NERVES,
I'M COMING APART AT THE SEAM!"

"I HATE I EVER HAD YOU!"
MEAN THINGS I WOULD YELL
THE BRUISES ON HER LEGS,
I DARED HER NOT TO TELL.

I SLAMMED HER IN THE CHAIR,
WHAT AN AWFUL THING TO DO.
A POOR DEFENLESS CHILD,
ALL BLACK AND BLUE.

I THOUGHT I WAS DOING RIGHT,
OH WELL, WHAT'S THE USE;
I DIDN'T UNDERSTAND,
IT WAS REALLY CHILD ABUSE.
THIS IS MY CHILD,
I THOUGHT I DID NO HARM,
UNTIL THAT LITTLE INOCIENT CHILD,
LAY LIFELESS IN MY ARMS.
"OH LORD," I CRIED,
FROM THIS COLD DARK CELL,

LISTEN VERY CAREFULLY
TO WHAT I HAVE TO TELL.

NOW AS I THINK BACK,
THE SAME THING WAS DONE TO ME.
CAUSED FRUSTRATION, HEARTACHE
AND A LIFE OF MISERY.

THERE WAS FEAR IN MY EYES,
I HAD LOW SELF-ESTEEM.
LIVING A NORMAL LIFE,
SEEMED ONLY A DREAM.

GOD PROTECTED ME,
HE ALLOWED ME TO LIVE,
A LIFE IS NOT YOURS TO TAKE,
AND NOT YOURS TO GIVE.

IF YOU CAN'T HANDLE THE STRESS,
AND THE PRESSURES THAT LIFE
WILL BRING YOUR WAY,
CRY OUT TO GOD,
HE WILL HEAR EVERY WORD YOU SAY.

HE WILL LEAD YOU AND GUIDE YOU,
TO SEEK THE HELP YOU NEED,
HE HEARS OUR EVERY CRY
HE ANSWERS EVERY PLEA.

YOUR CHILD IS A PRECIOUS GIFT,
SENT FROM GOD ABOVE,
HE GAVE YOU A GIFT
TO CHERISH,
TO CARE FOR AND TO LOVE.

DON'T MAKE HER PAY FOR
WHAT SHE DOES NOT UNDERSTAND,
PROBLEMS ON THAT JOB,
OR IS IT THAT MAN?

DON'T ABUSE THAT PRECIOUS GIFT,
SHE LOVES YOU SO MUCH,
ALL SHE NEEDS IS A SMILE,
AND A WARM LOVING TOUCH.

I CAN STILL HEAR HER CRYING,
IN THE STILL OF THE NIGHT.
LAYING IN THE DARKNESS,
WITH NO HOPE IN SIGHT.

"MOMMIE I LOVE YOU,"
SHE PRACTICED IT SO WELL,
NOW I'M SOBBING AND CRYING,
IN THIS DARK LONELY CELL.

PLEASE HEAR MY WORDS.
"GOD WILL FORGIVE,
LOVE THAT CHILD, TEACH HER,

AND ALLOW HER TO LIVE."
"ENCOURAGE HER,
AND DO YOUR JOB WELL,

DON'T END UP LIKE ME,
IN A DARK LONELY CELL."

HOW CAN I SAY THANK YOU

HOW CAN I SAY THANK YOU
WHEN THE ROAD SEEMS DARK AND
I'VE LOST MY WAY,
WHEN MY BILLS ARE DUE,
AND I CAN NOT PAY.

FAMILY TRIALS
CAUSE HEARTACHE,
AND MY LOVE ONES GO ASTRAY,
WHEN MY DREAMS ARE BROKEN,
DISAPPOINTMENT COMES MY WAY.

WHEN I'M TALKED ABOUT
AND I KNOW IT'S NOT TRUE,
NO ONE KNOWS THE PAIN
I GO THROUGH.
I WANT TO RESPOND
IN A CHRIST LIKE WAY,
WHAT DO I DO?
WHAT DO I SAY?

WHEN I'M WALKING ALONG,
AND STEP ON A NAIL,
ALL I DO SEEMS TO FAIL.
THE WORDS WON'T COME
AND I CAN'T EVEN PRAY,

I SEE TROUBLE AND DISPAIR
DAY AFTER DAY.

NOTHING EVER SEEMS TO GO RIGHT,
I'M TIRED OF THE TRIALS
I'M TOO WEAK TO FIGHT.
"HOW CAN I SAY THANK YOU LORD
WHEN LIFE SEEMS SO UNFAIR,
THE BURDENS, THE PAIN, ARE HARD BEAR?"

"HAVE I DONE SO MUCH WRONG,
THAT GOD WON'T FORGIVE ME OF?"
I CAN'T FEEL HIS MERCY AND I'M NOT SURE
OF HIS LOVE.
WHERE ARE YOU GOD?
HAVE YOU FORGOTTEN ME?
ALL I'M GOING THROUGH,
LORD CAN'T YOU SEE?

I PRAYED AND PRAYED,
THEN HEARD HIS ANSWER TO MY PLEA.
"TAKE YOUR EYES OFF YOURSELF,
AND PUT THEM ON ME."
"SIMPLY LOOK AROUND,
SOMEONE WORSE OFF CAN SURELY BE FOUND."

"VISIT THE HOSPITALS AND NURSING HOMES,
COMFORT SOMEONE WHOSE
LOVE ONE IS GONE."

"VISIT THE HOMELESS
TAKE THEM FOOD TO EAT,
OFFER A BLANKET,
AND A WARM PLACE TO SLEEP."
"VISIT AN ORPHANGE,
HUG A MOTHERLESS CHILD,
TAKE THEM A PRESENT,
GO THAT EXTRA MILE."

"LOVE THE PERSON YOU AVOID
WITH A NEEDLE IN HIS VEIN,
WHO CAN'T KICK THE HABIT
OF USING COCAINE."
REMEMBER GOD LOVES THEM TOO,
IT COULD HAVE BEEN ME,
IT COULD HAVE BEEN YOU.

"VISIT THE LONELY WIDOW,
SIT FOR AWHILE,
TURN THAT EMPTY FACE
INTO A SMILE."
"PRAY FOR THE PERSON WITH HIV,
FOR A MIRACLE FROM GOD
FOR THE WHOLE WORLD TO SEE."

OH LORD FORGIVE ME,
HOW SELFISH I'VE BEEN,
YOU DIED FOR ME
AND FORGAVE ME OF SIN.

YOU'VE KEPT ME AND BLESSED ME WITH PLENTY,
I REMEMBER THE WORDS OF EPHESIANS 5:20.
GIVING THANKS ALWAYS FOR ALL THINGS,
IN THE NAME OF OUR LORD JESUS CHRIST,
BEFORE I COMPLAIN, I'LL ALWAYS THINK TWICE!

EVERYDAY IS THANKSGIVING
NOT JUST ONCE A YEAR,
GOD HAS HEARD MY CRY
AND BOTTLED EVERY
TEAR.

THERE'S NOTHING I CAN DO
OR NOTHING I CAN SAY,
THAT COULD EXPRESS
MY THANKS TO GOD
FOR THE PRICE, HE CHOSE TO PAY!!

Gladys Kneeland © Copyright protected October 2005

I CAN SEE

I CAN SEE THE HOMELAND AFRICA,
WHERE THE CHILDREN WOULD LAUGH AND PLAY
THEY WERE VERY HAPPY THERE,
THAT'S WHERE THEY WANTED TO STAY.
THE BIG SHIP ON THE WATER
TOOK THEM FAR FROM THEIR
NATIVE LAND
BOUND THEM AROUND THE NECK,
CHAINS ON THEIR LEGS AND HANDS.

I CAN HEAR THE CHAINS CLINGING
LOUD AND CLEAR,
I CAN SEE THEIR EYES FULL OF HORROR,
PAIN AND FEAR.
I CAN HEAR THE WHIPS,
AS THEY TEARS FLESH FROM THE BONE,
THE PRIDE OF THE KINGS OF AFRICA WAS LOST,
ALL HOPE WAS GONE.

I CAN SEE THEM IN A STRANGE LAND
WHERE THEY DIDN'T ASK TO GO
WHO ARE THESE ANGRY PEOPLE
THAT WE DON'T EVEN KNOW?

I CAN HEAR THAT MOTHER CRYING,
"PLEASE.......
DON'T TAKE MY CHILD AWAY,"
CRYS THAT WENT IGNORED
ANOTHER SON WAS SOLD TODAY.

I CAN SEE THE COTTON FIELDS
WHITE AS NEW FALLEN SNOW
BODIES BENT IN HEAT,
AS THEY MOVED FROM
ROW TO ROW.

I CAN HEAR THE VOICES SINGING
DEEP...... AND LOW,
"GO DOWN MOSES
TELL PHARAOH
LET MY PEOPLE GO."

I CAN HEAR THEIR QUESTIONS
"WHO IS DIS JESUS DAT DEY CANNOT SEE,
WHO IS DAT MAN DEY SAY
WILL SET THE CAPTIVE FREE?"
"WHO IS DIS JESUS DEY SAY
WILL TAKE YOU BY DA HAND,
GIVE YOU BRAND NEW LIFE
LEAD YOU TO DA PROMISE LAND?"

I CAN HEAR THEM PRAYING,
IN THE MORNING,
AND LATE AT NIGHT
"LORD, SAVE OUR PEOPLE,
WERE JUST TOO WEAK TO FIGHT."

I CAN HEAR GOD'S ANSWER,
"I BROUGHT YOU FAR ACROSS THE SEA,
NOW YOU CAN KNOW A LIVING GOD
DRAW NIGH AND CLOSE TO ME."

"I WILL RAISE UP YOUR PEOPLE
BRING YOU FROM THE COTTON FIELD,
PUT FOOD ON YOUR TABLE
GIVE YOU A DECENT MEAL."
"I WILL CEASE THE HAND
OF EVERY VIOLENT ACT,
BRING YOU OUT OF SLAVERY,
TAKE THE WHIPS OFF YOUR BACK."

I CAN SEE THOSE FACES
THAT WE HAVE ALL COME TO KNOW
FREDERICK DOUGLAS, HARRIET TUBMAN,
AND W.E.B. DU BOIS.
THE STRUGGLES HAVE BEEN HARD
AND THERE'S STILL MUCH WORK TO DO
MARTIN LUTHER TRIED
NOW IT'S UP TO ME AND YOU!

SLAVERY HAS CHANGED ITS WAYS
IT HAS A NEW DISGUISE, BUT ITS PLANS COMES TO
LIGHT WHEN OUR YOUNG PEOPLE DIE.
DRUGS, GANGS, AND VIOLENCE
THEY PLAGUE OUR CITY STREETS,
GRABBING OUR BOYS AND GIRLS
WITH A FORCE THAT'S HARD TO BEAT.

HAVE WE FORGOTTEN DIS JESUS
DAT WE CANNOT SEE,
DAT BROUGHT US OUT OF SLAVERY
DA ONE DAT SET US FREE?
DIS JESUS DAT TOOK US BY DA HAND,
GAVE US BRAND NEW LIFE
GAVE US STRENGTH TO TAKE A STAND!

"LORD, SAVE OUR PEOPLE,
WE'RE JUST TO WEAK TO FIGHT,"
WE PRAY IN THE MORNING
AND VERY LATE AT NIGHT.

I CAN HEAR GOD'S ANSWER
AND IT'S STILL THE SAME.
"I CEASED THE LYNCHING
TOLD YOU TO CALL MY NAME."

"I BROUGHT YOU THROUGH
VIOLENT MARCHES,
IN EVERY STRUGGLE

I KNEW YOUR PAIN,
TRUST IN MY WORD
IT STILL REMAINS THE SAME."

"I WILL RAISE UP YOUR PEOPLE,
I WILL SET THEM FREE IF YOU CALL ON A
LIVING GOD
DRAW NIGH AND CLOSE TO ME!!"
I CAN SEE, I CAN SEE.

CHANGE

THE VISION STARTED
VERY LONG AGO
THERE SHOULD BE A CHANGE.
WOULD SOMEONE MAKE A DIFFERENCE
OR WOULD THINGS REMAIN THE SAME?

A SENATOR FROM CHICAGO
WALKED THE STREETS,
HE HEARD THEIR VOICE
HE LISTEN WHEN THEY TALKED
YES, THEY SHOULD HAVE A CHOICE.
HE KNEW WHAT IT MEANT TO BE POOR
HE FELT THEIR HURT AND PAIN,
TO MAKE THIS NATION BETTER THERE SHOULD
BE A CHANGE.

HE HEARD THE NATION'S CRY
RED, YELLOW, BLACK AND WHITE,
HE PONDERED IN HIS MIND
HOW CAN I MAKE IT RIGHT?
JOBS GONE AND HOMES LOST TOO
HOW CAN I HELP?
WHAT CAN I DO?

NEW IDEAS, NEW HOPE, BRAND NEW STARTS
WORK TO MAKE A CHANGE;

A DREAM IN HIS HEART.
THE ROAD WOULD NOT BE EASY,
IT WOULD BE AN UPHILL FIGHT,
HE STAYED FOCUSED,
AND KEPT THE DREAM IN SIGHT.

HE HAD DETERMINATION,
HE GATHERED ALL THE BEST,
HE HAD HIS WIFE'S BACKING
NOW HE COULD STAND THE TEST.

HE WOULD NOT GIVE UP THE RACE
WITH THE NATION ON HIS MIND
HE IGNORED ALL THE NAYSAYERS
AND LEFT THE PAST BEHIND.

FAME, GLAMOR, GLITTER, SURROUNDED HIM
EVERY DAY,
HIS FIGHT WAS TO CHANGE THE NATION,
HE WAS NOT DISTRACTED ALONG THE WAY.

NO MATTER WHAT YOUR PEDIGREE
NO MATTER WHERE YOU LIVED
HE FOUGHT TIRELESSLY
GAVE THE BEST HE COULD GIVE.

DOUBTED BY POLITICAL PUNDITS,
SOMETIME CRITIZED BY HIS OWN
AT TIMES HE EVEN WONDERED

WAS HE IN THIS FIGHT ALONE?

PACKING AND UNPACKING
TRAVELING FROM TOWN TO TOWN,
HE MET PEOPLE WITH A SMILE AND SOME
WITH A FROWN.
HE ENCOURAGED HIMSELF
HE SAW THE BATTLE THROUGH,
HISTORY WILL BE WRITTEN
WITH A FUTURE FOR OUR CHILDREN TOO.

AT LAST THE RACE WAS OVER
THE NATION MADE THEIR CHOICE,
THE DREAM BECAME
A SHOUT OF VICTORY IN THEIR VOICE.

THE MOMENT WAS EXHILARATING!!
UNRESTRAINABLE JOY
TEARS ON THE FACE OF EVERY
MAN, WOMAN, GIRL AND BOY.

AS WE LOOK TOWARD THE FUTURE
WE ARE HEADED FOR A CHANGE
A NEW LEADER IN THE WHITEHOUSE...
BARACK OBAMA IS HIS NAME!!!

Written by Gladys Kneeland
701 S. GRETTA AVE.
WAUKEGAN, IL 60085
November 9, 2008

TEENAGE LIFE

IF BEING A TEEN
IS JUST A DREAM,
THEN WAKE ME UP
BEFORE I SCREAM.

****

"BE IN THIS HOUSE BY QUARTER TO NINE,
 DON'T BE LATE,
 BETTER BE ON TIME!"

"CLEAN THAT ROOM,
 IT LOOKS A MESS,
 PICK UP THOSE CLOTHES,
 AND HANG UP THAT DRESS."

"DON'T LEAVE THIS HOUSE LOOKING LIKE THAT,
 AND WHERE IN THE WORLD DID YOU GET THAT HAT?"

"GET OFF THAT PHONE,
 YOU AIN'T TALKING NOWAY,
 WHEN IT'S OFF THE HOOK,
 I HAVE TO PAY!"

"TURN DOWN THAT MUSIC,
 IT'S TO LOUD,
 BETTER PASS THAT TEST,
 AND MAKE ME PROUD!"

"TAKE OUT THE GARBAGE FROM YESTERDAY,
 CAN'T YOU HEAR A WORD
 I SAY?!"

"DON'T HANG WITH THOSE KIDS,
 THEY AIN'T NO GOOD,
 MAKES IT LOOK BAD
 FOR THE NEIGHBORHOOD!"
"AND WHERE IN THE WORLD
 DID THEY GET THEM CLOTHES,
 AND DON'T COME HOME WITH A
 RING IN YOUR NOSE!!"

"LORD…. HAVE MERCY,
 WHERE HAVE YOU BEEN,
 LOOKING LIKE SOMETHING
 THE CAT DRUG IN?"

"NO! YOU CAN'T DRIVE MY CAR,
 WALK TO SCHOOL,
 IT AINT THAT FAR."

"I'M THE ONE IN CHARGE OF THIS HOUSE,
 I BROUGHT YOU IN,
 AND I'LL TAKE YOU OUT!"

"TURN OFF THAT GAME,
 WHAT'S WRONG WITH YOU,
 AND MAKE SURE

YOUR HOMEWORK'S THROUGH."

"WATCH YOUR LITTLE BROTHER,
TILL I GET BACK."
YAKETY, YAKETY, YAKETY YAK!!
****
YOU LEAVE YOUR HOUSE
AND HEAD TO SCHOOL,
TO FOLLOW
ANOTHER SET OF RULES.
YOU TRY TO SMILE,
SO IT WON'T SHOW,
BUT YOU'RE DESPRESSED,
AND FEELING KIND OF LOW.

THE CLASSES ARE HARD,
YOU'VE DONE YOUR BEST, BUT STILL DIDN'T PASS
THE HISTORY TEST.

NO ONE LISTENS.... WHEN YOU HAVE
SOMETHING TO SAY.
OH WELL,
IT'S NOT IMPORTANT ANYWAY.
YOU DIDN'T GET PICKED,
DIDN'T MAKE THE TEAM,
THAT REALLY HURT YOUR SELF- ESTEEM.

YOU'RE THE ONLY ONE NOT WEARING
DESIGNER CLOTHES,
AND YOUR MOM WON'T LET YOU PIERCE YOUR NOSE.

YOU'RE TEASED AND LAUGHED AT
CALLED A JERK,
FOOD DUMPED ON YOUR
GOOD HOMEWORK.

SOMEONE HANDED YOU A PILL,
SAID SWALLOW THIS DOWN,
IT'LL HELP YOU CHILL.

YOU THOUGHT HE SAID HE WAS YOUR FRIEND,
BE BY YOUR SIDE TILL THE END.

WHAT IN THE WORLD IS GOING ON?
AND WILL I MAKE IT,
TILL I'M GROWN?
****
THIS MAY NOT BE THE BEST TIME OF YOUR LIFE,
BUT JUST CHILL OUT
AND HOLD ON TIGHT.

NEVER GIVE UP,
AND NEVER GIVE IN,
RUN THIS RACE
AND RUN TO WIN!

YOU TELL YOURSELF,
IT AIN'T HIP AT HOME.
BUT YOU CAN MAKE IT,
JUST BE STRONG.
AT TIMES YOU THINK,
FORGET THIS SCHOOL
BUT DON'T BE TRICKED,
DON'T BE NO FOOL.

SO DRY YOUR TEARS,
DON'T YOU CRY,
THE YEARS WILL PASS SO QUICKLY BY.
YOUR FUTURE IS BRIGHTER THAN YOU CAN SEE,
SO LIVE YOUR LIFE AND
JUST BE FREE.

YOU SAY NO ONE KNOWS
OR FEELS YOUR PAIN,
MANY WALKED THAT ROAD,
AND HURT DON'T CHANGE!

NOW THIS IS ALL I WANT TO SAY.....
GET BY YOURSELF AND START TO PRAY.
CONFESS THOSE FEARS,
NAME THEM ALL.
GOD WILL HEAR YOU WHEN YOU CALL.
AND WHEN EACH NEW
DAY BEGINS,
PRAY FOR STRENGTH

TO HELP YOU WIN.

SO WELCOME TO YOUR TEENAGE YEARS,
IT'S NOT A DREAM,
SO CALM YOUR FEARS.

AND WHEN YOU'RE GROWN,
YOU'LL LOOK BACK.
IT'LL BE YOUR TURN TO: YAKETY, YAKETY,
YAKETY YAK!!

PASTOR JAMES & DEBORAH LOGAN

<u>JUST WANT TO THANK YOU</u>,
FOR ALL THAT YOU HAVE DONE.
YOU'VE PRAYED FOR OUR DAUGHTERS,
YOU'VE PRAYED FOR OUR SONS.
YOU'VE PRAYED FOR OUR FAMILIES,
WHEN THINGS WEREN'T GOING RIGHT,
WE CALL YOU IN THE MORNING,
AND VERY LATE AT NIGHT.

<u>JUST WANT TO THANK YOU</u>,
FOR ALL THE GOOD YOU DO,
PREACHING THE WORD OF GOD,
IT HELPS US MAKE IT THROUGH.
PUTTING UP WITH ATTITUDES,
THAT SOMETIMES AREN'T THE BEST,
BUT GOD GIVES YOU STRENGTH
CAUSE HE KNOWS IT JUST A TEST.

YOU LABOR FOR THE KINGDOM,
FEEDING ALL THE SHEEP,
NOT JUST ON SUNDAYS,
BUT EACH DAY OF THE WEEK.
ATTENDING EVERY MEETING
SPREADING YOURSELVES SO THIN,
PASTOR DEBORAH TEACHING WOMEN,
PASTOR JAMES TEACHING MEN.

JUST WANT TO THANK YOU,
FOR YOUR LABOR OF LOVE,
YOUR DILIGENCE AND PATIENCE,
THAT COMES FROM UP ABOVE.
WE CORNER YOU FOR HOURS,
BUT YOU DON'T WALK AWAY,
YOU LISTEN SO INTENTLY TO WHAT WE HAVE TO SAY.

SOMETIME MORE THAN ONCE,
SOMETIME MORE THAN TWICE,
WE HOLD ON TO YOUR PRAYERS,
AND CHERISH YOUR ADVICE.

FOR EVERY WEDDING YOU PERFORM, FOR EVERY
SERMON YOU PREACH,
LINE UPON LINE,
ON WEDNESDAY NIGHTS YOU TEACH.
THE COUNSELING YOU DO,
VISITING THE SICK AND THE SHUT-IN TOO.
COMFORTING FAMILIES,
WHEN THE OCCASION IS SAD,
THEY MAY HAVE LOST A MOTHER,
A CHILD OR A DAD.

JUST WANT TO THANK YOU,
AGAINST THE ENEMY, YOU TAKE A STAND,
CASTING OUT ALL EVIL,
LAYING ON OF HANDS.
ANOINTING US WITH OIL,

PLEADING JESUS BLOOD;
FASTING AND PRAYING
FOR EVERY NEIGHBORHOOD.

SOMEONE CALL THE PASTOR,
BUT IT'S TWELVE O'CLOCK AT NIGHT!
A BROTHER FROM THE CHURCH
IS BEATING UP HIS WIFE!

MY DAUGHTER IS HAVING A BABY!
LORD, CALL THE PASTOR QUICK!
SOMEONE'S IN THE HOSPITAL,
I THINK THEY'RE VERY SICK.

PLEASE CALL THE PASTOR,
MY SON IS GOING TO JAIL!
TELL HIM TO PRAY FOR US,
WE NEED TO RAISE THE BAIL!

WE NEED TO CALL THE PASTOR,
OUR RENT IS WAY PAST DUE,
THE CUPBOARD IS BEAR
AND THE KIDS NEED SHOES.

OUR LIST COULD GO ON,
BUT WE'VE RUN OUT OF TIME,
SO MANY BURDENS TO BEAR,
SO MUCH ON OUR MIND.

WE COULD BUY YOU GIFTS,
BUT THEY WOULD FALL APART,
THE THANKS THAT WE GIVE
IS COMING FROM OUR HEART.

WE SEE THE POWER OF GOD,
AND HIS SPIRIT MOVING TOO!
GLORY HALLELUIAH!!
THANK GOD FOR SENDING YOU!!

THE LONG JOURNEY

THE SCREAMS AND MOANS WOKE ME
THE CHAINS HELD ME TIGHT,
THE DARKNESS FILLED MY EYES,
THERE WAS NO HOPE IN SIGHT.

WHAT CRIME HAD I COMMITTED?
WHY WAS I FORCED TO GO?
HOW LONG IS THE JOURNEY,
AND HOW WOULD I KNOW?

LOOKS OF HOPELESSNESS
ON EACH FACE
FEAR IN THEIR HEART
IN THIS UNFAMILIAR PLACE.

PANGS OF HUNGER GRIPPED MY STOMACH
I LONGED FOR MY NATIVE LAND,
THE SMELL OF ROTTEN FOOD
FED BY A STRANGERS HAND.

THE STENCH MADE ME GAG,
THE TEARS STANG MY EYES,
WILL THIS JOURNEY EVER END
OR WILL IT BE MY DEMISE?

I SANK TO THE FLOOR
TRIED TO DROWN THE PAIN
TRIED TO KEEP MY SANITY,
KEEP FROM GOING INSANE.

HOURS TURNED TODAYS
DAYS TO WEEKS,
WEEKS TO MONTHS,
WILL THE TORTURE EVER END?
WHERE IS MY FAMILY
WILL I SEE THEM AGAIN?

MEAN WORDS SHOUTED AT ME
I DID NOT UNDERSTAND
I WAS MOVED BY EMOTION
AND THE WHIP IN THEIR HANDS.

I HEARD SLPASHES ON THE WATER,
AS BODIES WERE THROWN TO THE SEA,
I TURNED MY HEAD AND SHUTTERED,
THE NEXT COULD BE ME.

THE JOURNEY STARTED LONG AGO
BROUGHT MY PEOPLE TO A DIFFERENT
SHORE,
NOT KNOWING WHAT LIES AHEAD
OR WHAT WAS IN STORE?

SOME OF US MADE IT, AND SOME HAD TO DIE,

I WILL NEVER KNOW THE REASON,
BUT ALWAYS WONDER WHY.
I BELIEVE GOD HAD A PLAN
FAR BEYOND WHAT
I WILL EVER UNDERSTAND.

ENCOURAGE YOUR CHILDREN,
TO BE ALL THEY CAN BE
REMIND THEM OF THE SUFFERING
MADE FOR YOU AND ME
ON THE LONG JOURNEY.

'TIS THE SEASON

'TIS THE SEASON …
CHRISTMAS IS IN THE AIR
THE EXCITEMENT OF HOLIDAY SHOPPING
GIFTS AND PRESENTS TO SHARE.
HEARTS FILLED WITH JOY,
WE'VE BOUGHT THE LATEST GADGET FOR EVERY
GIRL AND BOY.
THE HUSSLE AND BUSSLE, SHOPPING MALLS,
THE CROWDED GROCERY STORE,
ARMS FILLED TO THE BRIM WITH
PACKAGES GALORE.
PLACES TO GO, THINGS TO BUY,
THE SKY'S THE LIMIT, NO PRICE TO HIGH.

'TIS THE SEASON…
DECORATIONS SPARKLE ON HOUSES,
ORNAMENTS HANGING FROM TREES,
OFFICE PARTIES, GALAS, SO MANY PEOPLE
TO PLEASE.
DECK THE HALLS, CROWDED CITY STREETS,
"MERRY CHRISTMAS!" SHOUTED
TO EVERYONE WE MEET.

'TIS THE SEASON…
FAMILIES COMING TO VISIT
PAINT THE WALLS, CLEAN THE CARPET

MAKE EVERYTHING LOOK NEW,
LITTLE TIME LEFT, AND STILL SO MUCH TO DO.
TURKEYS AND HAMS ADORN THE TABLE
CAKES, COOKIES AND PIES,
OPENING GIFTS AND PRESENTS
DELIGHT FILLS OUR EYES.
LAUGHTER, JOKES, HUGS AND KISSES TOO,
A GIFT OF EXTRA POUNDS,
WAITING FOR ME AND YOU.

SPORTS BLASTING FROM THE DEN,
WOMEN HUDDLED AND PLANNING
LET'S DO THIS AGAIN.

'TIS THE SEASON…
TO REMEMBER THE LESS FORTUNATE,
HELP TO BRING ABOUT SOME JOY,
BUY AN EXTRA GIFT FOR A HOMELESS GIRL AND BOY.
NO CHRISTMAS TREE WITH SPARKLING LIGHTS,
NO VISIT WITH SANTA, NO HOPE IN SIGHT.
THE JOBLESS MOTHER WITH FIVE MOUTHS TO FEED,
WHO WILL COME TO HER RESCUE,
HELP MEET HER NEED?
SHE FALLS ON HER KNEES IN THE QUIET OF
THE NIGHT.
"FATHER BLESS MY CHILDREN, I'M JUST TOO TIRED
TO FIGHT."

THE FATHER GIVEN A PINK SLIP, HE'S FEARFUL, AND
AFRAID; WONDERING WHERE HE WENT WRONG AND
WHAT MISTAKES HAD HE MADE?
HOW CAN HE PROVIDE FOR HIS FAMILY?
WHAT ON EARTH CAN HE DO?
HE PRAYS A SILENT PRAYER,
"LORD HELP SEE US THROUGH."

'TIS THE SEASON...
WHEN THE BROKEN HEARTED AND LONELY,
HAVE FEELINGS OF GREAT DESPAIR,
THE PRISON CELLS NO CALL FROM HOME
SEEMS NO ONE REALLY CARES.
THE FEELING OF CONDEMNATION,
GUILT AND SHAME,
HIS VOICE ABOVE A WHISPER
HE CALLS ON JESUS NAME.

'TIS THE SEASON...
TO VISIT HOSPITALS AND
NURSING HOMES TOO,
WE ARE THE MASTERS HANDS,
THERE'S MUCH WORK TO DO.
SING A CHRISTMAS CAROL BRING A SMILE TO A
WEARY FACE, THANKFUL TO GOD,
WE'RE NOT IN THEIR PLACE.

'TIS THE SEASON...
CHRIST CAME TO SAVE US,

TO GIVE KNOWLEDGE OF SALVATION UNTO HIS
PEOPLE FOR THE REMISSION SIN,
FOCUS ON HIS GRACE AND MERCY,
NOT GIFTS AND PRESENTS FROM MEN.
SING "OH HOLY NIGHT,"
REACH OUT TO YOUR NEIGHBOR,
BE THAT BEACON OF LIGHT.
SHOW LOVE, GIVE A KIND WORD,
A SERMON LIVED MAYBE BETTER
THAN ONE THAT'S HEARD.

'TIS THE SEASON...
GAIN A LOST SOUL, BE A TRUE FRIEND!
GLORY TO GOD IN THE HIGHEST
PEACE ON EARTH;
GOOD WILL TOWARD MEN!!!

Love and Peace,
Gladys Kneeland

GOD WROTE THE SCRIPT

"BEFORE I FORMED YOU IN THE BELLY,
 I KNEW YOU."
"I HAD ALREADY WRITTEN THE YOUR SCRIPT;
 THE PART I CHOSE FOR YOU,
 NO ONE ELSE WOULD FIT."

"BEFORE I FORMED YOU IN THE BELLY,
 I KNEW YOU."
"THE CURTAINS BEGAN TO RISE
 I KNEW ALL THE YOU WOULD DO,
 YOUR LAUGHS, YOUR SMILES, YOUR CRIES."
"THE STAGE –
 WAS ALREADY SET,
 THE PARTS YOU WOULD REMEMBER,
 THE PARTS YOU WOULD FORGET."

"BEFORE I FORMED YOU IN THE BELLY,
 I KNEW YOU."
"I KNEW THE ROLL YOU WOULD PLAY,
 I KNEW THE MISTAKES YOU WOULD MAKE,
 I KNEW EVERY WORD YOU WOULD SAY."

"I KNEW WHAT WAS AHEAD,
 I KNEW YOUR NEXT SCENE,
 SOME PARTS FUN,
 SOME WERE CRUEL AND MEAN."

"SOME PARTS WERE OF LACK,
SOME WERE OF WEALTH,
SOME WERE OF SICKNESS,
SOME WERE OF HEALTH."

"BEFORE I FORMED YOU IN THE BELLY,
I KNEW YOU."

"I CRIED WHEN YOUR PART WOULD UNFOLD,
TRIALS, HEARTACHES AND PAIN
WOULD CRIPPLE YOUR VERY SOUL."
"I KNEW YOU'D BE TRIED,
AND PUT TO THE TEST,
I WROTE THE SCRIPT,
I KNEW WHAT WAS BEST."
"I KNEW SOMETIMES YOU WOULD BE NICE,
SOMETIMES YOU WOULD BE MEAN,
REMEMBER, I WROTE THE SCRIPT
I KNEW EVERY SCENE."

"I KNEW YOU WOULD POUT,
WHEN YOU WERE CHASTEN,
IT WOULD HELP YOU TO GROW
I KNEW WHAT YOU WOULD PLANT,
I KNEW WHAT YOU WOULD SEW."
"BEFORE I FORMED YOU IN THE BELLY,
I KNEW YOU."
"I KNEW WHO WOULD COME INTO YOUR LIFE
I KNEW THE PART THEY WOULD PLAY,

I KNEW WHO WOULD GO,
I KNEW WHO WOULD STAY."

"BEFORE I FORMED YOU IN THE BELLY,
 I KNEW YOU."
"I KNEW WHAT YOU COULD HANDLE
 AND WHAT YOU COULD BEAR,
 I KNEW YOU WOULD CRY,
 LIFE ISN'T FAIR."
"I KNEW WHAT YOU WOULD TAKE,
 I KNEW WHAT YOU WOULD GIVE,
 I KNEW WHERE YOU WOULD TRAVEL,
 I KNEW WHERE YOU WOULD LIVE."

GOD IS IN CONTROL; HE'S IN THE DIRECTORS CHAIR
HOLD TO YOUR FAITH,
IN YOUR DEEPEST DESPAIR.

CONSULT HIM AND BE LED BY HIS POWERFUL HAND,
WHEN FACING THOSE PART YOU DON'T UNDERSTAND.
HE IS THE POTTER; WE ARE THE CLAY
WE'RE SAFE IN HIS ARMS,
HE WON'T CAST US AWAY.
THIS SCRIPT WAS DESIGNED ESPECIALLY FOR YOU,
NOT YOUR SISTER OR BROTHER,
NO ONE ELSE WOULD DO.
WHEN THE PART IS LONG, AND NEVER SEEMS TO END,
HIS PLAN WON'T BE ABORTED,
SO DON'T WORRY,

WE WIN.

IF WE BLOW ONE SCENE,
BECAUSE WE MADE A MISTAKE,
HE ALREADY KNEW
AND WILL DO ANOTHER TAKE.
WHEN WE LEAVE IT TO HIM,
JUST RELAX AND DO OUR PART
REMEMBER HE WROTE THE SCRIPT
HE KNOWS THE END FROM THE START.

REMEMBER GOD WROTE THE SCRIPT,
NO ONE ELSE COULD
HE'S MAKING YOU STRONG,
IT'S WORKING FOR YOUR GOOD.
STRAIGHTEN YOUR SHOULDERS
KEEP MOVING FORWARD,
FOR YOUR ROLE YOU'LL RECEIVE
AN ACADEMY AWARD!

I WILL NEVER FORGET

I WILL NEVER FORGET
THE LAUGHTER AND JOY.
THE HAND I HELD SO GENTLY,
LIKE A LITTLE GIRL AND BOY.

I WILL NEVER FORGET
THE PLEASURE OF HOLDING HIM IN MY ARMS.
GETTING INFORMATION,
HIS INTELLIGENCE AND CHARM.

I WILL NEVER FORGET
NEW EXPERIENCES
HE INTRODUCED ME TO.
THE WARMTH OF HIS KISSES
LIKE SUNSHINE ON THE MORNING DEW.

I WILL NEVER FORGET THE MAN I LOVE,
SO UNCONDITIONALLY,
WHEN HE MADE ME SMILE, IT JUST SET ME FREE.
JOY IN MY HEART TOOK AWAY THE FEAR,
I WILL CHERISH EACH PRECIOUS MEMORY
FOR THE REST OF MY YEARS.

THE LOVE AND MEMORY OF THAT MAN,
I WOULD SHOUT IT FROM THE ROOFTOP,
FOR ALL THE WORLD TO HEAR,
BUT I'VE LOCKED IT IN MY HEART,
TO HOLD FOREVER NEAR!

Printed in the USA
CPSIA information can be obtained
at www.ICGtesting.com
CBHW071109030324
4918CB00013B/1077

9 781498 439374